Education make you fick, innit?

What's gone wrong in England's schools, colleges and universities and how to start putting it right

the Tufnell Press,

London,
United Kingdom

www.tufnellpress.co.uk

email contact@tufnellpress.co.uk

British Library Cataloguing-in-Publication Data
A catalogue record for this book is
available from the British Library

ISBN   *1872767 672*
ISBN-13   *978-1-872767-67-3*

Copyright © 2007 Martin Allen and Patrick Ainley

First published March, 2007
Second edition May, 2007

Printed in England and U.S.A. by Lightning Source

Education make you fick, innit?

What's gone wrong in England's schools, colleges and universities and how to start putting it right

Martin Allen and Patrick Ainley

Epigraph

'Twenty years of schooling and they put you on the day shift'

Bob Dylan

Invitation

If you would like to join a discussion about the ideas raised in this book or related matters please go to

http://radicaled.wordpress.com/radicaled-home-page/

Introduction

What has gone wrong

England's state schools, colleges and universities have shared the fate of other public services as the post-war welfare state was at first slowly expanded and then, from the late-1970s on, disbanded with accelerating rapidity. However, compared with other public services, education remains unique in the way it has been integrated into the more general economic and social policies of successive governments. This is not only because of the contradiction involved in privatising—ultimately making the public pay for—legally compulsory school attendance, as well as for extended further and higher education and training thereafter.

This book argues that institutionalised 'learning' in England's schools, colleges and universities, together with training in and for work, has come to play an increasing part in social control. In a daily more divided society, whole groups of people are relegated to permanent unemployment and many more to permanent insecurity in employment. Official 'learning' for longer and longer periods substitutes for the guarantee of regular wages in integrating many employees into a changing economy. Dedicated obsessively to the vocational 'needs' of the economy, education, whether in school, college or university, no longer aspires to emancipate the minds of future generations. Instead, it is increasingly foreclosing possibilities. In this sense, *Education Make You Fick, Innit?*

In tracing how this has come about and suggesting what can be done about it, this book charts the paradoxical growth of both state control over schools, colleges and universities and competition between them. The new approach was announced back in 1976 by declaring an end to the previous comprehensive school reform. In its place, a new settlement of education and training was eventually imposed by the 1988 Education Reform Act, together with the 1992 Further and Higher Education Act.

The integration of this new system of education with training has since gone much further under New Labour governments, especially their 2006 Education and Inspections Act. Yet the White Paper preceding this Act suggested government desperation as an ICM opinion poll coinciding with its launch showed two thirds of parents did not consider schools any better than under the

Conservatives. Later in the year, international comparisons by the Organisation for Economic Cooperation and Development (OECD)'s *Education At A Glance 2006* showed the UK falling in comparison with education indicators of other developed countries. More recently, the House of Commons Public Accounts Committee of cross-Party MPs reported that 'the education of almost one million children is suffering because they attend schools that perform badly' (*Observer*, 8 October 2006). Standards would not be raised by 'inappropriate methods and targets', according to the independent *Nuffield Review* the same month.

As evidence piled up that, after ten years of frantic activity, things were still not going right in education, the concerns of Blairite politicians were more immediately felt by large numbers of teachers and lecturers. They faced the problem of what to do during what Willis in 1977 described as an 'endless succession of Monday mornings' and they have drawn similar conclusions, albeit for very different reasons! For many students also, going to school, college, or university has become a daily grind, where much of their 'learning' appears irrelevant to the increasingly complex demands they face from society.

Signs of their dissatisfaction are familiar to the teachers who have to respond to them. School truancy at record levels is the most common of these symptoms but at the most extreme, 20 schools a week (400 a year) are targets of arson attacks (*Guardian*, 4 April 2006). Yet at the same time, for the most examined and certified generation in history, with more and more jobs demanding higher and higher qualifications, 'education' matters more than ever before. So, according to the Department for Education and Skills, about 80 per cent of 16 year-olds remain in school or college, while around 42 per cent of 18-30 year-olds go on to higher education (47 per cent of women but only 37 per cent of men).

The main argument of this book is that the 'success' or 'failure' of all this education cannot be explained simply in terms of the inadequate design of its internal structures or through problems with implementation, even if nobody should question the fundamental importance of these areas. It connects changes in education and training and the relation between them to wider changes in society. Particularly important is the vexed question of social class and its recomposition over the last half century. This affects also the altered gender balance of occupations and relations as well as the situation of various minority ethnic groups. All are involved in perennial debate over the place of the vocational compared with the academic.

How to start putting it right

A central thesis of the book is that it is not too late to reclaim and reshape education. The resistance against the 2006 Education and Inspections Act could signal a changing tide in the battle for an education that encourages real learning and understanding, extends culture and democracy and in increasingly uncertain times aims at sustainability in place of increasing social division and ultimate self-destruction. This book seeks to encourage that process by offering an accessible explanation linking together schools, colleges and universities in a coherent account.

Part of the explanation for failure to recognise *What has gone wrong* and *how to start putting it right* lies in the isolation of teachers in primary from secondary from further from higher education. This is seen not only in the parochial concerns of each sector and the way they recurrently blame each other for the failings of the system as a whole but in our narrow professional and trade union organisation, as well as the limited focus of academic research and debate. The recent merger of the two further and higher education unions to form the University and College Union is a step in the right direction.

The book is therefore intended firstly for teachers in primary and secondary schools, together with those teaching and researching in higher education and also further education. It seeks to enable them to compare their daily experience with that of others in other parts of what we argue is now an interconnected education and training system that has to be grasped in its totality to be understood. The book aims to overcome divisions between the different sectors of state education and relates also to the (growing) private sector, including private training.

The book is therefore also aimed at students in college and university trying to make sense of their experience as the first generation expected to pay so much for what has become mass tertiary level learning, having already been 'tested to destruction' in primary and secondary schooling. Trainee teachers too are key readers for whom the book will provide essential background understanding. Other specialist students, lecturers and researchers in education studies and cognate subjects, including the sociology, psychology, politics and philosophy of education will also hopefully find the book valuable.

However, although academically rigorous, this is not written as an academic text. References—most of them for this introduction in this paragraph—are kept to a minimum, for instance. Unlike recent excellent studies of the education policy process (Chitty, 2004a), or the history of it (Jones, 2003), and the updated second edition of Sally Tomlinson's *Education in a post-welfare society* (2005), this book is not primarily for academics and their students. Nor is it concerned to describe the situation of just a part of education today—usually schools, as in Benn and Millar's 2006 campaigning pamphlet for *A Comprehensive Future*, or Terry Wrigley's *Another School is Possible*. These accounts do not relate what has happened in schools to the rest of education and training. Similarly, Mary Evans' elegantly written *Killing Thinking* (2004) deals only with higher education.

It is important to link not just the sectors of education that are often treated separately but also other related areas, such as training, social security, family and youth policy. These are covered from the perspective of youth work in Phil Mizen's 2004 *The Changing State of Youth*. Phil's title highlights changes in the state itself as well as in public services and their new relations with the private sector. He argues, and we agree, that these have led to a crisis of legitimacy for the new market-state. One of its responses has been an extension of social control through education, its tests, examinations and certification. As a result there has been, as Phil writes (p. 41), 'a huge expansion in education's influence over the lives of the young.'

We therefore disagree with much of the academic explanation of change in education. Typically this sees 'the development and dissemination of a *global policyspeak*' (Ball forthcoming) as somehow determining events. This sort of 'discourse analysis' cannot explain why events happened when they did (and not sooner or later, for instance). Nor does it grasp the education and training system as a whole in the wider context of which it is a part.

Unlike the books above, though, our account of education is restricted to England, while recognising that devolution within mainland UK to Scotland and Wales has allowed space for the creation of at least partial alternatives to the crisis-ridden English dead end. These alternatives may grow more divergent as they build towards rejecting the English model in whole rather than in part. This account of the recent development of education in England can therefore be taken as a negative example or awful warning to readers elsewhere. Our comparisons with international developments illustrate this. They expand the explanation of what has gone wrong to connect it to the educational agenda of international bodies to which the UK and EU are signed up, such as the World Bank, the World Trade Organisation and, in particular, the WTO's 1994 General Agreement on Trade in Services (GATS).

"The bamboozling of a generation"

There is a growing general realisation, shared especially by those without any vested interest in the growth of education and training, that the expansion of 'lifelong learning' and all the emphasis put upon it and 'foundation learning' in schools by successive governments over the past 30 years has not led to greater knowledge and enlightenment. Instead, we suspect what the great French educational sociologist, Pierre Bourdieu once called, *The bamboozling of a generation* as education looms larger than ever before in the lives of young people and in the concerns of their parents. This concern is seen in widespread allegations of what is incorrectly called 'dumbing down' (also incorrect because being unable to speak does not necessarily imply stupidity). These allegations have paradoxically but not coincidentally accompanied the recent expansion of and emphasis on education.

We explore this paradox, drawing upon the two authors' own experience, previous research and publication. We offer a diagnosis that does not fall into the simplicities of genetic, psychological or political reduction. Instead, we give an explanatory narrative that is clear and comprehensible but without simplification. Unlike many other books that have detailed the workings and implications of education policy, we address the crucial issue of what sort of alternatives are required to restore public confidence in education and to make it enjoyable and worthwhile. Most importantly, our concern is with how education can regain its purpose of handing on the expanding body of human knowledge for new generations to build a sustainable future.

As far as we know, the human species is unique in being able to learn not only from our own individual mistakes but from the collective account of human and natural history and science. In this sense our species can be characterised, as William Morris said, as 'the learning animal.' Yet control over organised social learning is being relinquished to the competitive global economy to which its whole purpose is now dedicated. This is happening at the same time as the ecology that sustains human life is being disrupted by the unconstrained expansion of that same global economic competition. This could be considered as 'ecocidally insane' and the opposite to any kind of learning from experience to alter behaviour in the future. How English education came to contribute to this collective insanity and what can be done to change it is detailed in the chapters that follow. The argument is necessarily compressed in the following section of this introduction.

Outline of the book

Chapter 1

The opening chapter charts the issues that will reverberate throughout the book. It reviews current thinking about education, economic performance and social progress, to identify a number of contradictions. For example, on the one hand governments have given education a major new role in securing national economic survival in a global marketplace. They have also emphasised education's importance in encouraging greater democracy and participation. On the other hand, education has been used to both maintain divisions between and to limit the capacities and aspirations of many of the young people it now puts in academic competition with one another. To resolve this contradiction, the chapter examines how changes within the workplace have led to a recomposition of the class structure and, as a result, to changes in the relationship between education and training/skill formation. It asks whether, in an age of information technology, divisions of knowledge still reflect differences in power; and why some educational credentials continue to be worth more than others. Finally, it discusses what it now means to be 'qualified' and whether this is necessarily the same as being 'educated'?

Chapter 2

The second chapter describes how the expansion of education in the post-war years both reflected and supported economic expansion, but also accommodated rather than challenged many of the historical inequities and 'peculiarities' that have been a feature of English society. For example, why was it that England, the first industrial country, trailed behind other developed countries in the creation of a system of public education? The 1944 Education Act, for example, belatedly introduced free secondary education for all. But it also replicated wider social divisions of labour and knowledge by dividing young people on the basis of spurious psychological tests into the tripartite system of state secondary schooling. At the same time, the domination of the élite private schools was preserved linked via their exam boards to admission to the antique universities. The chapter argues that even though the 1944 Act represented a significant marker in the long process of educational reform, it also failed to energise popular support for increasing educational opportunities in the period of post-war reconstruction.

The chapter then moves on to examine how the comprehensive reformers of the 1960s and the progressive primary practitioners of the 1970s struggled in face of an unequal playing field—an educational terrain still dominated by the privilege and élitism of the surviving grammar and private schools—and how as a result, in many areas, the comprehensive ideal remained embryonic. The chapter argues that instead of being a 'failure' in the way that 'bog standard' comprehensives you 'wouldn't touch with a bargepole' have been portrayed by both the Conservatives and increasingly by New Labour, it is to their credit that comprehensive schools managed to achieve as much as they did.

Alongside the child-centred primary schooling that could flourish once the age of selection was raised from 11-to 16-plus (although it soon dropped back to 14), comprehensive schools established a legacy that politicians since have been unable to directly deny. As a result, even Blair/Brown and Cameron today are forced to repeat that 'There will be no return to selection' as a result of their proposals. Instead of such a return, the comprehensive ideal of 'equal opportunities' has been perverted by Mrs. Thatcher's translation of it into 'opportunities to be unequal.' Twenty years on, this perversion of the comprehensive principle is seen in the lip-service education ministers pay to 'individual and personalised' learning with 'inclusion for all.'

While it begins by emphasising the importance of education in supporting economic prosperity, the chapter concludes by providing an insight into how the fortunes of education, and particularly its progressive and comprehensive aspirations, were undermined by deteriorating economic conditions. It examines how Labour, the political party most associated with educational expansion, faced with unfavourable economic conditions during the 1970s, increasingly cast schools and teachers as responsible for hampering economic recovery rather than as catalysts of progress. Indeed, Prime Minister Callaghan in calling a halt to Old Labour's policy of comprehensive reform actually blamed teachers for not producing 'employable' workers, thus scape-goating schools and colleges for an economic recession and unemployment for which they had no responsibility.

This 'Big Lie' was repeated many times during the succeeding phase of education policy that we call (following Finn) *Training Without Jobs*. By contrast, in criticising the subsequent and continuing subservience of education to 'what employers want'—even whilst many employers continued to lay off workers and deskill many of their remaining employees through automation—the chapter points towards a realistic assessment of the part that education to all levels can play in contributing to sustainable economic development.

Chapter 3

After defeating resistance by organised workers who included not only the miners but teachers engaged in prolonged industrial action over pay, successive Conservative governments went on to 'roll back the state' and privatise nationalised industries and welfare provision as a way out of economic recession. In this context, the 1988 Education Reform Act (ERA) imposed a new settlement on English schooling. It moved from the national system locally administered of the 1944 welfare-state settlement towards a national system nationally administered through contracts to meet targets in what was becoming a new market-state.

As responsibility was contracted out to a periphery of 'agents' and 'providers' like schools and colleges, power contracted to a central core. The ERA reduced the powers of democratically accountable Local Education Authorities (LEAs) by delegating budgets to schools and, more significantly, gave them the option of leaving local authority control completely. It also made a 'National' Curriculum compulsory in all state—but not private—schools in England (Wales, in a significant concession, gaining its own version—Scotland always had its own independent education system). In another of the perversions of the comprehensive principle that this book records, this National (and in history and other remaining subjects, Nationalist) Curriculum was sold to teachers as a comprehensive entitlement for all their pupils but in which league tables compared their results in Standardised Assessment Tests for 5, 11 and 14 year-olds and in GCSEs at 16.

The ERA was complemented by the 1992 Further and Higher Education Act which 'incorporated' the further education and sixth form colleges as independent bodies in competition with one another for students. They followed the polytechnics in establishing their independence from LEAs and became dominated by a new funding regime tied to student numbers. The justification for this was that it would 'free' the colleges from the dead hand of bureaucratic LEA control but, as was to happen with the same process in schools and higher education, the result was a new centralised state bureaucracy following an incomprehensible funding formula while recreating little bureaucracies within each institution, thus multiplying 'red tape' overall.

In a process which was later to be inflicted on schools and then higher education, college staff also became subjected to inspection and direction by a variety of external quality auditors and inspectors. This regulation initiated a new education and training market for further education as a plethora of competing

Youth Training Schemes were made compulsory for the rising numbers of jobless school leavers. The chapter concludes with a brief explanation of how the market in trainees and students determined provision in the competition that now infects the entire system from primary to postgraduate schools.

Chapter 4

Chapter four takes us to the present and to the latest 2006 Education and Inspections Act. New Labour elevated education to an unprecedented position even compared with Mrs. Thatcher who abolished the rival Department of Employment. She had dropped the welfare state commitment to full employment so that there was no longer any economic policy other than opening markets to global competition. Instead, the merged Department of Education and Skills (once Education and Science) was charged with securing 'employability' for new entrants and re-entrants to the labour market. Meanwhile 'Science'—significantly for the future of state-sponsored research—was hived off to the Department of Trade and Industry. Education and training also appear as the main instruments of social mobility (even as this is reducing), thus preserving illusions of 'meritocracy'—that all jobs are open to anyone irrespective of their social background and that opportunities if not circumstances remain equal for all.

At the same time, education and training has been assigned a leading role in the 'active labour market policies' to reform the welfare state urged on successive governments by international bodies such as the OECD and other representatives of globalising corporate capital. Aimed at meeting the demands of intensified global economic competition and using new communications and information technology (ICT), such policies also involve handling the 'social exclusion' of a section of the traditional manual working class left behind as the welfare state has contracted and the social deprivations following upon this economic restructuring have multiplied.

Forcing young people from 'deprived'/discriminated against backgrounds into an education that has systematically failed and excluded them from the earliest ages is inherently contradictory. As a result of retaining, rather than challenging, these key Conservative policies and because of the importance given to appeasing those who have benefited from economic restructuring, rather than protecting those who have lost out, New Labour has presided over continuing and heightened inequities in education as in society as a whole.

In schools this reality can no longer be hidden by what the government calls its 'standards agenda' and the faltering Literacy and Numeracy Strategies. In fact, the system of perpetual crisis management policed by the Inspectorate has driven schools into an impasse from which the 2006 Act presented independent trust status on the City Academies model as the only way out but without the funding to sustain it. This is an invitation to the private sector to move into the provision of public education in line with the European Union commitment to the General Agreement on Trade in Services, though whether this private provision of public services happens more or less immediately may depend on local circumstances. The same commitment to privatisation is taken further in the accompanying 2006 Further Education White Paper with its proposals for private provision and voucher-style arrangements for funding. The raising of student fees in September 2006 also aims to create a market in higher education.

In post-compulsory education and training the concept of 'lifelong learning' has become central as it supposedly builds upon the 'foundation learning' of those in primary and the early years of secondary, even though this 'foundation' is increasingly inappropriate for what would previously have been recognised as in any sense 'higher' education (if only for a minority). For those (mainly boys) who are not sent to college or even to work on 'apprenticeships' at 14 and for whom an alternative 'work-based route' has repeatedly failed to replace the old apprenticeships that finally collapsed along with heavy industry in the 1980s, 'widening participation' offers the substitute of a mass higher education. 'Experience of higher education' is intended to be available to fifty per cent of 18-30 year-olds by the end of the decade—a target that has already been achieved in Scotland but which will not be achieved in England (unless 'higher education' is redefined as 'higher education but not as we know it'!)

As well as being contradictory with the aspiration to widen participation to social groups hitherto under-represented in higher education, raising student fees instead of progressive income tax to fund university expansion has led to the intensification of traditional hierarchies already entrenched under Conservative governments. Divisions within and between the élite Russell Group of universities and other institutions, particularly those given university status after 1992, have also been reflected in divisions between 'researching', 'teaching' and 'training' universities. In the latter, competence-based courses, like many of the two-year Foundation 'degrees', remove the independent and critical thinking supposedly characteristic of higher education.

At the same time as higher education is thus turned into further education, parts of further education may be renamed 'higher' as further education follows the 2005 Foster Report recommendations for a new tertiary tripartism separating academic sixth forms from technical centres of vocational excellence and generalist 'skills' colleges. Further education was given a new role by the 2006 White Paper *Raising Skills, Improving Life Chances* of 'equipping young people and adults with the skills for productive, sustainable employment in a modern economy.' So a narrow focus on vocational so-called 'skills' relegates the mass of students attending further education to work-related training programmes. For many, these will begin at 14 with vocational diplomas dictated by employer-run Sector Skills Councils. This is the government's *Skills Strategy*. Typically, Foster also recommended the private take-over of 'failing' colleges that New Labour has encouraged for schools and LEAs. 'LearningFare' for second language learners, those with special educational needs and others failed by the increasingly academically selective system may then be the only free (if compulsory) courses available.

There are now eight and a half million full-and part-time students and trainees in the UK. The Learning and Skills Council claimed to be funding six million learners in sixth forms, colleges and training schemes in and out of employment in 2004-5. In addition, there are nearly two million Higher Education Funding Council funded undergraduate students with half a million more postgraduates at the 2003 maximum. They are paying more and more for less and less as terms become shorter and classes larger in increasingly chaotic and virtual universities.

As further and higher education fees rise, mergers and closures of colleges and universities can be anticipated while the uncapping of the initial £3,000 limit on student fees may allow the 'Magic Five' universities (Oxbridge, Imperial, UCL and LSE) to privatise themselves out of the system by setting their own fees for different courses accountable to no one but the market. Despite limited bursaries, entry to different levels of further and higher education will then transparently be linked to ability to pay in the worst of both worlds—a mass higher education for the many combined with an élite higher education for the few.

Chapter 5

Although many of New Labour's education policies represent a move away from the comprehensive ideal back towards the 1944 system of tripartism and selection, the changes in class, occupation and workplace reorganisation that they are responding to are not unique. Neither are some of the particular policy initiatives that have been introduced. For example, the publically funded independent schools in Sweden have been cited as the inspiration for trust schools outlined in the 2006 Education Bill, while the plans for specialised vocational education from age 14 are, government claims, modelled on practices elsewhere in Europe. U.S. influence has of course also been pervasive in a country derisively referred to as the 51st State of the Union ever since Mrs. Thatcher's embrace of Reaganomics.

This chapter set the previous narrative in this wider context. It relates the 'neo-liberalisation' of education to economic arguments for a so-called 'knowledge economy' and how this is reflected in the desires of successive UK governments to privatise and outsource significant parts of the education system and to allocate educational resources through 'market' principles rather than those of equality and social justice. Thus in England, first further education and the polytechnics were removed from local education authorities to compete for students, then higher education fees were introduced and then raised to create a market in students and now schools are being set 'free' to become responsible for their own admissions of students/pupils. Despite the attempts by opponents of the 2006 Act to limit this last move, at all levels of learning the ensuing competition is leading to merged institutions, closed departments and intensified teaching.

This process of what Colin Leys called 'market-managed consolidation' is happening despite increased funding. We will show that money has been spent ineffectively—on inspection and target-chasing by centralised agencies, rather than being given to schools, colleges and universities to use as they know best. For what is the use of the Chancellor's largesse if the extra money goes to consultancies and private partners in PFIs/PPPs, or is poured into Academies sponsored by businessmen in return for peerages and/or the privilege of indoctrinating pupils in 'creationism'? This is state-sponsored privatisation where the only equality between state and private will be when both are private. It is prompted not just by the urgency of Prime Ministerial pressure or concern for his 'legacy' but to meet the timetable set by the US-dominated WTO for transnational investment in education in this round of the GATS together with continuing European integration along 'free market' lines.

So this chapter exposes these real reasons behind Blair and Brown's 'modernisation' and Cameron's support for it. The commitment of both main Parties is to privatise the remaining public services, following Mrs. Thatcher's denationalisation of industries, transport and communications in the 1980s. New Labour's 'modernisation' of education thus accompanies Post Office privatisation, together with what remains of NHS dentistry and the reintroduction of the internal market to hospitals with money following patients, just as it does students in higher education, further education and, since the 2006 Act, schools.

Chapter 6

The concluding chapter of the book is perhaps the boldest in that it confronts the difficult task of constructing alternatives. Here it is unlike most other recent accounts of education, many of which have provided rigorous critiques but have held back from promoting remedies. Preceding chapters refer to the opponents of particular policies—striking school teachers and lecturers, anti-SATs campaigners, the National Union of Students and the Campaign for Free Education, journalists critical of government spin, researchers evaluating particular policies, parents opposing Academies, Liberal-Democrat and Nationalist opposition in Parliament joined by Labour back-benchers and Green and other national and local opposition. There has indeed been resistance but it has remained fragmented. What has yet to be developed is an alternative project as coherent and as wide ranging as New Labour's neo-Thatcherism, one that seeks to 'join up' the fragments of dissent and produce a distinct and viable alternative.

By way of a contribution to this task, the chapter outlines clear alternatives in the areas where New Labour has been seen to have failed. It draws upon a range of policy documents about curriculum and assessment practice produced by organisations like the National Union of Teachers and the National Union of Students, together with statements of intent from campaigning bodies across all sectors of education. It thus seeks to answer the question 'what is education for?' in ways that many other authors have avoided and it argues why, irrespective of its importance to economic performance, education does indeed still matter (Wolf, 2002). It distinguishes between an educated society and one that is schooled or merely 'certified' (Ainley 1999).

Finally, it seeks to intervene in those areas of policy where New Labour have enjoyed a monopoly and where progressives have had little to say. For example, it addresses the issues of 'personalised learning' in schools and further education with its use of ICT to promote learning. It opposes blaming the groups of young people who are failed by predominantly academic schooling and exposes their relegation to 'vocational' routes in training and education and to more restrictive social control in other aspects of their lives. It confronts accusations of 'dumbing down' in higher education and argues for 'free' rather than 'free market' universities and colleges. It contrasts education in and for citizenship with education for consumers in relation to a multicultural society and global sustainability. It does not claim to provide a definitive alternative in the shape of a blue-or even *Redprint for Education (Hillcole, 1991)*. But it will have served its purpose if teachers and students at all levels of learning can act upon the ideas and proposals it presents to restore and extend the sustainable education needed to contribute to human survival in the future.

Chapter 1

The big picture—Education and economy

This opening chapter addresses the social and economic changes that have provided the context for the development of English education policy over the last twenty years and more. The chapter is critical of many of the arguments used by recent governments to justify the introduction of these new policies, particularly those concerning the economy, qualifications and skill formation. It provides an alternative explanation through which these relationships can be better understood.

Education, economy and society in the post-war years

The expansion of state education after the second world war was closely aligned with the recovery of industry and the programme of social reconstruction which accompanied it. Although education and training continued to be organised in different ways in different countries, there was general agreement across Western governments that education should be seen as a form of investment. According to what became referred to as 'human capital theory', education and training were regarded as investment goods. Like increases in the stock of physical capital such as plant and machinery, investment in education represented increases in the stock of 'human capital.' Therefore the benefits of more education to both the individual and society were indisputable.

Human capital theory was extremely general in its claims. For example, rather than seeking to identify and prescribe in detail what should be learned and how, it emphasised the importance of education as a whole in promoting the economic welfare of society. This was particularly significant in post-war Britain, where both Labour and Conservative governments continued to promote the expansion of schooling, while at the same time allowing teachers considerable professional autonomy over what happened in classrooms. While central government continued to define the overall level of resources for education, Local Education Authorities (LEAs, the education committees of locally elected borough and county councils) had powers to determine the exact levels of expenditure in their schools and colleges and for administering most of the service. But if, in Britain at least, the central state took a back seat within what was called the post-war, welfare state 'consensus' and was content to allow education to be run by its local partners, education still continued to reflect wider assumptions about the post-war economic and social order.

For example, as a result of the 1944 Education Act, the state secondary schools introduced to complement the primary schools that together replaced pre-war elementaries were organised through a tripartite system of grammar, technical and secondary modern schools. These divisions reflected deeply held assumptions about the nature of the production process, its skill requirements and also the aptitudes of those who worked in industry. They represented a concession to the popular pressure for better and fairer education for all at the same time as limiting that demand to supplying labour for rebuilding Britain's factory mass production.

A minority (approximately twenty per cent) of young people who passed an 11-plus 'IQ' test progressed to grammar school, though this was harder if they were girls because the test was weighted against them (as in Northern Ireland until recently). They might then, though this was even harder for women, go on to a future career in business, commerce, or one of the traditional professions providing the backbone of the (still small) non-manual, office/white-collar workforce. An even smaller minority followed this route via three additional years at university (approximately two per cent of 18-21 year-olds, overwhelmingly male pre-war, though more than trebling to 7.2 per cent by 1963 with a growing female minority). Those considered to have a 'technical' aptitude were similarly intended to provide the skilled labour force required for post-war reconstruction (though the numbers progressing to technical schools never exceeded 4 per cent and trade training therefore continued through apprenticeships with day-release to college at best—rising to about 40 per cent of male school leavers by 1968). Finally, those whose future employment would not (as the Ministry of Education circular number 73 acknowledged) require any technical skill or particular knowledge, attended one of the new secondary modern schools before leaving for un- or semi-skilled employment.

Thus, despite the post-war political commitment to social reconstruction and increasing opportunity across society, the connection between education and future occupational destiny was established at an early age. In addition, the private schools with their intimate links to élite higher education were 'shunted into a large siding' as the architect of the Education Act, 'RAB' Butler, put it and forgotten about thereafter. There was therefore in the minds of politicians and their civil servants a deliberate correspondence between the state school system and the existing divisions of labour in the economy. As noted, this was vitiated by the failure to build enough of the more expensive technical schools and so skills training was displaced into what was to become Further Education supporting traditional apprenticeships through day-release from work.

The education and training system also partially corresponded with the inherited 'upper', 'middle' and 'working' class structure of society. Whilst these traditional divisions were consolidated in the 1950s by the corresponding institutionalisation of learning, eventual change in the 1960s and thereafter was driven not only by popular demand but by new technology and by the recomposition of the class structure, as well as by the loss of the protected markets of empire. Education and training (or learning) policy then aimed at constructing a new correspondence with the economy and society. But comprehensive reform from 1965-76, through the 'new vocational' phase of *Training Without Jobs* from 1976-88, on to the contradictory academic expansion after 1988 that created what we call 'Education Without Jobs', to the latest implementation of the 2004 *14-19* White Paper proposals for new vocational lines of learning in the 2006 Act, all repeatedly failed to achieve this impossible goal of 'bridging the skills gap' to give employers exactly what they wanted from education.

For example, the gradual move from a divided grammar and secondary modern state school system towards comprehensive education from the 1960s onwards was, as chapter two will emphasise, spearheaded by a powerful lobby of reformers committed to social justice and equality of opportunity. However, it is unlikely that the campaign for comprehensive education would have achieved the results it did, had there not been a growing consensus across the political spectrum that in a developing economy, all young people, rather than just those in the grammar school minority, needed to be educated to a much higher level. It was not simply that the economy was growing, it was also the case that the occupational structure itself was changing. Not only would blue-collar manual workers need much higher levels of skills in the future, it was argued they would increasingly give way to a growing white-collar workforce. In the 'white heat' of Prime Minister Wilson's promised 'technical and scientific revolution' physical drudgery would be replaced by automation and laboratories as the catalysts of economic growth.

There were indeed major changes taking place in the composition of the workforce. Women, for example, were returning to the workforce in greater numbers and more middle-class women were opting for careers instead of housewifery. Meanwhile, although apprenticeships faltered, emigration of skilled workers to the former white dominions of the Empire allowed of some continuing upward mobility within the manually working class as the place of semi-and unskilled workers was taken by immigrants from the largely Black and Asian New Commonwealth. The move towards comprehensive secondary schools was intended not only to assimilate these new arrivals but mainly to prepare young men and women for modernised production as a means to social equality by overcoming the manual/non-manual class division between the traditional working and middle classes.

Comprehensives took the pressure of preparing pupils for 11-plus selection off primary schools that could then experiment in the creative, 'child-centred' education advocated by the Plowden Report (HMSO, 1967). Comprehensives were also accompanied by an expansion of further and higher education with the creation of new technical universities and polytechnics specialising in science and technology alongside the new universities recommended by the Robbins Report (HMSO, 1963). Significantly though, piecemeal and incomplete structural comprehensive school reform was not accompanied by reform of the academic curriculum dictated by the exam boards and the élite universities. As a result, the comprehensives competed on an uneven playing field with the surviving grammar and private schools to get their pupils into academically selective higher education. Nevertheless, 'the end of selection' at 11-plus was established by Old Labour government in 1965 as a principle it would be hard for future governments to renege on and impossible for politicians to advocate openly since selection of the few clearly failed the majority.

These developments were not only 'modern', they also reflected a new spirit of classlessness and a renewed optimism about the openness of society. Education was seen as helping to create a 'meritocracy' in which an individual's position was achieved instead of being ascribed by the innate intelligence supposed by psychologically flawed 'intelligence' testing at an early age. Like comprehensive schools, expanded further education and the polytechnics—also under the control of democratically accountable LEAs—aimed to make it possible for working-class students to qualify for the professional occupations entered by those completing courses at universities. This expansion of opportunity was underwritten by the reality of employment in a growing welfare state together with state-supported modernisation of the economy. Yet, as the following chapter will argue, despite pressure to create a fairer society, the post-war

English education system continued to uphold tradition, defend privilege and promote inequality.

From consensus to crisis

1960s optimism about the levelling potential of education opening up possibilities of careers for all in place of dead-end jobs for most was soon extinguished. The end of the 'long boom' of thirty years full employment since 1945 followed war in the Middle East and an Arab oil boycott that precipitated international recession in the mid-1970s. Keynesian demand management of the economy by successive governments, Labour and Conservative, finally broke down. But instead of a debate on the economy, the Labour government launched a 'Great Debate on Education' that called a halt to its comprehensive reform. This followed Prime Minister James Callaghan's 1976 Ruskin College speech denouncing schools and colleges as responsible for poor national economic performance. Teachers were blamed for increases in youth unemployment considered to be the consequence of poor levels of literacy and numeracy and the 'unrealistic attitudes' of young people. As described earlier (p. 7) this 'Big Lie' has been repeated many times since. Yet it was employers—not teachers who employ no one, being themselves employees—who were laying off workers and not recruiting.

As traditional industrial apprenticeships collapsed along with heavy industry, employers increasingly expected state schools and colleges to take responsibility for training their workforce. They demanded government replace the emphasis given by educationalists to a free thinking 'liberal humanist' curriculum with one which for many students was to become directly related to the world of work. At the same time, centrally funded government agencies such as the Manpower Services Commission (MSC) bypassed democratically elected local authorities to enrol school leavers on Youth Training Schemes while funding work-related initiatives in schools, further education and later higher education.

These pressures resulted in changes in what was taught in schools, colleges and—eventually—universities. During the 1980s, a 'new vocationalism' emerged, the design of which was said to reflect changes in the organisation of the work place. Vocationalism appropriated the progressive critique that had been made of irrelevant academic education to put in its place behaviourally-defined and work-related 'competencies.' However, as chapter three will emphasise, this was just one example of how education and training were to be reshaped to reflect new economic realities. There was growing pressure on the education service to be brought to book in other ways. Teachers and lecturers, it was argued, not only needed to be more 'accountable', but in addition, as well as providing the training that employers demanded, schools and colleges had to be seen to deliver a consistent rise in academic standards.

The 1988 Education Reform Act marked a switch to what can be called 'Education Without Jobs' as school leavers—particularly young women—voted with their feet. They preferred to stay on at school or further education to progress to higher education rather than enter what Dan Finn called *Training Without Jobs*. In the schools sector the 1988 Act was designed to roll back the gains of comprehensive education, imposing an academic National Curriculum. Sold to teachers as an 'entitlement curriculum' for all pupils and thus as a further extension of the comprehensive ideal, it actually perverted that ideal through competition between schools for examination and test results.

The increasingly selective system was inspected and regulated by still more central and only indirectly accountable agencies that implemented a business model to create a leaner, more market orientated and more 'cost effective' schooling. Mrs. Thatcher rejected direct privatisation of state schooling through the vouchers that appealed to her Education Secretary, Sir Keith Joseph, but she saw the 1988 Act 'going further than ever before' to prepare the ground for the privatisation of education. She therefore reversed the previous tendency for the extension of state provision in relation to the private sector under previous Labour governments (even though Old Labour had rejected nationalisation of the private schools) and moved towards privatising the state schools.

Globalisation, education and New Labour

However, it was the election of a New Labour government in 1997 that signified going 'further than ever before' in education policy. The Tories had already abolished the Department of Employment, along with any attempt to maintain full employment or indeed any control over the economy that was now deregulated to the world market. New Labour privatised the Bank of England and took the political elevation of 'education, education, education' further as it substituted it for employment policy in an increasingly globalised but also more fragmented and unpredictable international economy.

It is with the contradictions and the insincerities of New Labour's education policies that we are primarily concerned. They represent a further perversion of the comprehensive ideal. Education in an increasingly academic and selective system was supposed to provide the human capital investment that would buy individual and national success in the global economy to which Mrs. Thatcher had opened the national economy. Her successive de-, or rather re-, regulations with a series of state-subsidised privatisations of formerly state-owned enterprises, followed the acceptance of International Monetary Fund conditions for loans accepted by the last Old Labour government in 1976.

As chapter four will confirm, debate about education policy has been part of a more general debate about how best to respond to these 'New Times.' Governments have adopted a neo-liberal economic agenda, in which, they argue, they can no longer guarantee full employment or the traditional forms of welfare provision. As the Organisation for Economic Cooperation and Development saw *The Future of Social Protection* in 1988,

> 'Changing economic structures and the growing challenge from more open trading systems increase the likelihood that unemployment will exist more as a consequence of structural changes than as a demand deficiency or frictional phenomenon. In these circumstances, social protection systems need to do more than simply provide income while the individual searches for employment ... Education and training are thus likely to become one of the main pillars of social security for tomorrow's citizens.'

Politicians and a compliant media typically claim that international capital is now so all powerful that the only alternative is for individuals as well as companies to acquire high stocks of human capital to assure their survival. Employment can thus no longer be guaranteed save by individuals, employed and unemployed alike, along with new entrants to the labour market, developing their 'employability' through perpetual education and training. In this way, education has been substituted for economic policy.

For critics of this new consensus, the consequences of globalisation mean that education is now part of a 'post-welfare' society in a 'new-market' state taking the form of 'a competitive enterprise and a commodity rather than a preparation for a democratic society' (Tomlinson, 2005: 1). And, like any other commodity, it has to be paid for—as now by higher education and adult students but not yet by school pupils for whom attendance remains legally compulsory to 16—18 in 2013 (though 14 in practice for many of those sent to college or training at work).

If globalisation is seen to have potentially negative consequences for economy and society unless the workforce becomes better qualified and more adaptable, government also argues that changes in the way production processes are now organised require specific changes to education. 'Fordist' production in heavy industry with standardisation, repetition and high levels of physical drudgery are, it has been argued for some time, being replaced by more flexible and demanding 'post-Fordism.' Gearing the economy to meet the individual needs of consumers encourages multi-skilling, allows more interesting and challenging work for more people and, as importantly, requires more harmonious relations between workers and management. For the proponents of post-Fordism, education has a particularly important role to play in developing the new 'collective intelligence' of 'a high skills economy.' In order to do this however, schools in particular must become less regimented, the curriculum must become more interdisciplinary and the relationships between teachers and students must be less hierarchical and more 'personalised.'

This optimistic version of post-Fordist thinking ignores the persistence of low skill and tedious employment, particularly in the expanded service sector of the economy. It also neglects the increasingly regimented conformity of target-driven schooling. Instead, advocates of such an approach see globalisation translated into more 'flexible', 'diverse' and 'personalised' learning with the increased use of computers in the classroom. The requirement for workers to be able to learn new skills once they have left education so as to protect themselves from the uncertainties of global competition, has led to a strong emphasis on promoting 'Lifelong Learning.' The new economic climate has also been used to justify what can be referred to as New Labour's 'standards' agenda. This has seen an aggressive campaign to raise general levels of performance in public examinations. Also, an obsessive emphasis on particular benchmarks, for example, the number of students meeting government literacy targets at age 11 and 14, the percentage gaining five A-C GCSE grades at age 16, the number remaining in school or at college to 18 and going on to higher education after that.

However, as part of the effort to maximise the potential of all young people and as part of attempting to change what New Labour have denounced as a 'one size fits all' model of 'bog-standard' comprehensive schooling, the government has also promoted increased 'diversity' of provision, with schools encouraged to apply for 'specialist' status. Learning has also become more diverse within schools following government advocacy of 'personalised learning' and the introduction of academic, vocational and work-based pathways from age 14 onwards. Heightened 'differentiation' of pupils following one of these three streams occurs from even earlier ages. Paradoxically this new tripartism, based upon testing what are in reality different levels of literacy, harks back to the lost world of the 1950s with its rigid class divisions of knowledge and labour.

The businessification of learning

Economic changes have also been cited as a reason for moving towards what New Labour policy makers have referred to as a 'post-comprehensive' model of education. According to New Labour, this demands fundamental changes to the 'culture' of education. As central government has appropriated their powers, leaving them only responsibility for local administration, there has been particular criticism of LE)As. These have been shorn of 'Education' by the 2006 Act to become just 'Local Authorities' supposedly responsible through Children's Trusts for integrating education with social and other services. They are accused of bureaucratic inability to provide the flexibility and innovative drive that schools now require—the same arguments that were used to strip democratically accountable LEAs of their former-responsibility for higher, further and adult education. Allegedly, this dynamism can only come from private entrepreneurs.

As a result, New Labour has continued with the Tory initiated process of outsourcing the running of schools. In a few cases this has led to the complete transfer of ownership to profit-making companies, or to the creation of public-private 'partnerships', but more often it has resulted in schools taken over by charitable or religious foundations. This trend has advanced furthest in the secondary school sector where New Labour has promoted the growth of 'independent' state schools in inner city and urban areas. These City Academies are financed by public funds but owned and controlled by business or religious sponsors. The 2005 White Paper *Higher Standards, Better Schools*, embodied in the 2006 Education and Inspections Act, contained proposals for all schools to become such independent and self-governing 'Trusts.'

Schools and colleges have also been encouraged to 'learn from business' in a number of other ways, particularly for their internal organisation. This has gone furthest in further education. There, as a result of the 1992 Further and Higher Education Act, college corporations under their Chief Executives have aped the private sector with funding tied to student completion rates. The new public management foisted on colleges and schools also compels them to follow this competitive regime of target setting and performance monitoring.

Funding schools, colleges and now universities according to the number of students, allowing 'popular' institutions to expand and threatening others with closure through the operation of supply and demand has created an internal market, where, just like in any other market, there can only be winners if there are also losers. As in business, failure to meet production targets can result in the sacking of management and even the closure or merger of the enterprise. Meanwhile, under another centrally imposed agency teams of 'quality control' OfSTED inspectors patrol the country searching for failing schools, colleges and LEAs. All this is supposed to have 'set schools and colleges free' from local authority control to meet parental, student and employer demand but actually it subjects them to an oppressive new bureaucracy.

The staffing structures of schools, especially large secondary schools, have also been changed. As previously in further education, New Labour have promoted a 'leadership' culture where 'school improvement' depends on the vision and managerial abilities of headteachers and their Senior Management Team rather than on the collegial practice of teachers. The increased autonomy or in some cases the 'independence' that schools have been allowed has, in many large secondary schools in particular, resulted in headteachers becoming Chief Executives, rather than educationalists, let alone teachers. This follows the example set by further education principals and the more entrepreneurial of university vice chancellors.

Not only have there been growing divisions between managers and managed, but the 'schools workforce', as the government refers to them rather than to 'the teaching profession', has become increasingly diversified with non-teachers being used to perform many of the duties that teachers have traditionally undertaken. Under 'workforce remodelling' or 'workforce reform', school support staff have taken on a number of administrative tasks that are not considered to require a teacher's 'professional judgement.' 'Higher level' teaching assistants have also been employed to provide cover for absent teachers or deal with student behavioural problems and to provide pastoral support.

The latest of successive reorganisations brings together local authority education with social services under Children's Trusts within which flexible staff can potentially be redeployed across formerly discrete professional areas of expertise. Services are 'integrated' to supposedly focus on the individual child by reorganising the workforce to operate within a common set of 'core skills' or competences with limited specialist skills and knowledge. This applies not only to teachers but to other formally autonomous professionals, such as social workers and youth and community workers.

Education, economy and society: a reappraisal

In view of these developments, the remaining pages of this chapter present a radically different view from the official and generally accepted one of the factors that have shaped education policy in recent years. We argue that many of the policies promoted by government have little direct link with increasing the economic welfare of UK plc or, indeed, of responding to parent or student 'choice'. On the contrary and in the context of the changing experiences of young people, they have been about increasing the use of education as a means of social control.

It is certainly the case that the demand for a closer correspondence between education and the economy has found its way into government policy statements in a significant number of countries. It is also true that trends towards both privatisation from above and businessification from within are marked in education systems worldwide. Nevertheless, the exact relationship between education and the economy remains a complex issue that raises as many questions as it answers.

Clearly, levels of education and skills amongst the workforce will always be an important factor in the economic performance of a country, but at best education can be seen as being but one of the major ingredients in a successful economy. A drive to 'raise standards' for example, cannot be enough in itself if at the same time there is an absence of high levels of investment, sound macro-economic planning and stable exchange rates. New Labour can therefore be accused of scapegoating education for the inadequacies of Britain's recent economic performance, just as Old Labour did under James Callaghan. But the attacks on education in the 1980s can be seen in the same light with, as chapter three demonstrates, much of the programme of Thatcher's New Right also having little direct relation to economic regeneration.

Despite regular surveys and complaints about 'skill shortages', it is not always clear which skills employers actually require. In Britain, the top employers' organisation, the Confederation of British Industry (CBI) used to emphasise the importance of 'creativity', 'team working' and 'problem solving' but now laments what it considers to be the poor level of basic skills. New Labour have assumed that the recent work-related focus of education will automatically translate into productivity gains and will win support from employers. Yet, as Glenn Rikowski has long argued, statements which attempt to define employer demands for youth labour are at best ambiguous and at worst 'downright contradictory.' As Glenn says, employers have always moaned about the educational shortcomings of the young people they recruit and in any case the present oversupply of certified if not qualified labour suits employers very well as it keeps wages low. Moreover, it is not as if employers are short of labour with UK unemployment rising towards two million again even on official figures (1.7 million at the last count).

In August 2006 as GCSE results were announced, the CBI once again criticised school-leavers for being insufficiently prepared for the world of work. This was based on research undertaken amongst 140 firms, sponsored by the Department for Education and Skills to find inadequacies in maths and English. As Glenn wrote in his educational comment blog, *The Volumizer*:

> 'The CBI Report could easily have been written in the 1970s or 1980s. Thus, after James Callaghan's Ruskin College Speech of 1976, the resulting Great Debate on Education, the 1988 Education Reform Act, ushering in the National Curriculum, national testing, SATs [standard assessment tasks], league tables, and then OfSTED, together with New Labour's focus on standards early on after 1997 and then the introduction of the Literacy and Numeracy Hours—school-leavers' reading, writing and maths are *still* inadequate for employers!'

Despite this fixation on spelling and times tables, arguments about globalisation suggest a certain logic to education's development. As production systems become increasingly similar it could also be assumed that educational development will become likewise. Yet there is no real evidence that the education systems of the most successful economies are actually converging, either in terms of what is learned or in the way in which it takes place. What continues to be significant is the part played by education in promoting national and cultural characteristics. As chapter three will show, the schools policies of the Conservatives during the 1980s and 1990s were as much about 'cultural restoration' as they were about economic modernisation. Rather than representing an effort to meet the challenge of globalisation and technical transformation, education policy during this period was both defensive and authoritarian.

Certainly the introduction of the National Curriculum as a result of the 1988 Education Reform Act cut short initiatives like the Technical and Vocational Education Initiative (TVEI), regarded by many as one of the boldest attempts at vocational modernisation. Instead, with a National Curriculum of ten academic subjects, all children would now be tested at the ages of 7, 11, 14 and 16, making English state school pupils the most tested in the world. As stated in chapters three and four, the linking of test and exam performance to league tables has meant that schools have devoted huge resources to ensuring that specific groups of children are taught to perform in particular ways in certain situations and that teachers 'teach to the tests.' In primary schools particularly, testing, especially of the final year 6, has once again turned teaching into the drudgery of cramming as children live in fear of the week of exams that they and most of their teachers all loathe at the end of the year.

So, while government and OfSTED claim they demonstrate constantly rising standards, many of those involved allege that these improvements are artificial. These allegations have recently been substantiated by research over a number of years by a team led by Michael Shayer, Professor of applied psychology at King's College, London. He concludes that 11 and 12 year-old children are 'now on average between two and three years behind where they were 15 years ago' in terms of cognitive and conceptual development (reported in *The Guardian* 24 January 2006 and forthcoming in *The British Journal of Educational Psychology*). In any case, international comparisons and league tables of test performances relate only indirectly and dysfunctionally to economic performance, with the currently dominant U.S. economy, for instance, being outperformed academically by countries with much weaker economies.

Technological or ideological?

Rather than being mistaken or ill-advised, we would argue that many of the motives behind education policy have been primarily ideological rather than technological in their intention. They appear as if they are a direct or inevitable consequence of globalisation and the resulting changes in production techniques but they transmit a message that because the world has changed, 'modernisation' of education along business lines is not only necessary but also inevitable. Thus, as Mike Cole observes:

'The spectre of globalisation is invoked by politicians and business people
as they seek to justify the diminution of the welfare state and the need
for the untrammelled expansion of the free market.'   (1999, 4)

Despite the rhetoric of government, it was the lack of employment
opportunities for school leavers and the inability of the Youth Training
Schemes of the 1980s to guarantee future employment that drove increases
in participation in full-time education during the last decade of the twentieth
century. It was not the introduction of a National Curriculum, as government
might claim, that raised staying on rates for 16 year-olds from 51.8 per cent
in 1988, when they were already rising in any case, to 80 per cent-plus today.
The brief introduction of unitary GCSE exams and the spread of more or less
comprehensive schools phasing out selection in large parts of England and in
all Scotland and most of Wales certainly helped to raise average attainment. But
the fact was there was no other option for most young people than to remain
in sixth form or go to college. This remains the case today now that this route
has become the norm for most young people.

It is true that increased staying on in education has resulted in significant
increases in examination performance with over half of the cohort now gaining
five GCSE grades at A-C as compared to 1970 and before when most left
school without any qualifications at all. Everybody welcomes this. But it is also
undeniably the case that employers have, as a result, increasingly demanded
higher levels of qualifications for jobs that previously did not need them. Thus
an endemic feature of modern labour markets has been a process of 'qualification
inflation' or 'diploma devaluation' in which the increases in entry requirements
for particular occupations are more a consequence of increases in the level
of qualifications held by applicants than they are of the increased technical
sophistication of the jobs themselves.

Unlike the proponents of human capital, for whom the increased level of
education by one individual contributes to an increase in the stock of educational
capital as a whole, we would argue that as increases in the level of educational
qualifications continue to outstrip increases in the technical sophistication of
production, this creates an escalator effect. The benefit gained by taking a few
steps up is then eradicated by the downward movement of the stairway as a whole.
As a result, people are running up a down escalator. For many school, college
and university graduates there is a lack of opportunity to use their educational

qualifications in the way that they hoped. Or in the way that previous generations with similar qualifications had been able to.

For the 1.7 million officially unemployed and the even larger numbers of insecure, part-time and contract workers, successive training schemes offer often illusory prospects of what in the past would have been described as 'proper jobs' with security, prospects, pension entitlements and paid holidays. Many adults in employment are training or retraining just to keep their jobs, often as a form of work discipline. This is not a qualified but a 'certified society', one where the qualifications that people hold may have only a limited relationship to the skill requirements of available employment.

Rather than confirming the acquisition of genuine skills and aptitudes, educational credentials serve as screening devices for employers. They enable certain types of applicants with certain types of qualifications to proceed to particular positions. They also allow employers and professional bodies to raise entry qualifications to neutralise the increases in the number of applicants with the previously required levels of credentials. This oversupply of certified if not qualified labour keeps wages low as qualifications perform a gate-keeping role for employment.

It is, however, ironic that, despite the criticism of academic education by their representatives, individual employers continue to recruit on the basis of success in qualifications that are considered to be the most academically prestigious. So, while employers officially deprecate academic qualifications in favour of their vocational equivalents, most of them give their top jobs to applicants with traditional A-levels or degrees from élite universities.

In other words, as well as providing prospective applicants with the means to enter particular occupational groups, educational qualifications also provide important functions for employers. But, just like monetary inflation in the real economy, the increasingly high pass rates in examinations like A-levels has intensified concerns about credential inflation, the value of particular qualifications, the status of particular institutions and the so-called 'dumbing down' of standards. One recent example of this trend can be seen in the way in which élite schools and the more prestigious universities and departments within them are setting their own entrance exams. They also want 'super starred A-levels' or the International Baccalaureate as a new 'gold standard' qualification in place of the now modular A-levels reorganised by the partial reforms of 'Curriculum 2000.'

Education and the recomposition of social class

Fundamental to our arguments about the increased significance of education in
social control is an on-going transformation of the occupational class structure
of Britain as well as other advanced capitalist economies. The remainder of this
chapter examines to what extent new divisions both within and between schools,
colleges and universities correspond with new divisions of knowledge and skill
in society and the economy.

How has the occupational class structure changed in recent years? Firstly, the
post-war social 'pyramid' reflected in the 1944 Act has pulled apart. This is not
only because the gap between richest and poorest has widened since 1976 (up
to which time it had been narrowing slightly but steadily in the 30 years before
then). It is also because in the traditional model, the most significant division
in the employed population was between manual and non-manual occupations.
This was invariably a division between those with academic qualifications and
those without.

It also remained the case that even though secondary education became
a universal provision after the 1944 Act, many working-class youth did not
identify with it and left school as soon as they could. They turned their backs
on the opportunities that state secondary education was supposed to provide
for upward occupational mobility. Indeed, the raising of the school leaving age
to 16 in 1972 was met with hostility by many working-class school students
and their parents anxious to exploit what was becoming an increasingly tight
labour market for school leavers.

However, the traditional working-class communities that supported types
of father-son succession, which Wilmott and Young in their classic 1957 study
of working-class family and kinship in East London described as a 'recognised
practice' and a sort of 'informal labour exchange', have also long disappeared.
The fact that traditional industries were invariably localised, meant that many
school leavers made what could be described as a 'collective transition' to work
with those they had been to school with. Today the transition from education to
employment not only takes much longer but it is also far more of a fragmented
and individual process.

Likewise the circumstances have changed which allowed Paul Willis in 1977
to follow a group of white working-class secondary modern boys through
their last months of compulsory schooling in Birmingham and into local
factory employment. They left school without qualifications but also with a

deep resentment towards education, its expectations and teachers, as well as a disdain for those pupils who tried to use it to achieve modest social mobility. 'The lads', as Willis fondly referred to them, did not need school to help them with *Learning to Labour*. The same cannot now be said for the large numbers of the current generation of 16 year-olds who are faced with a new type of labour market in which less than 15 per cent of the workforce are employed in manufacturing and where, at the beginning of the twenty-first century, more than 40 per cent of occupations can be officially described as 'administrative and managerial'/'professional and technical.'

We would argue that progression within an occupational order expanded from what used to be referred to as 'white collar' employment and associated with a minority 'middle class' now increasingly depends on gaining educational qualifications, rather than relying on what sociologists refer to as 'secondary' or internal characteristics to differentiate between potential employees. Most individuals seeking to enter the labour market do indeed now rely on qualifications to signal their 'skill assets.' These can be contrasted with 'organisational assets'—the advantages, skills and knowledge enjoyed over outside applicants by employees who have been able to establish themselves in relatively secure positions in an organisation compared with somebody just entering.

Yet if acquiring educational qualifications is a precondition for both gaining and being able to maintain secure employment, this does not mean that the occupational structure is necessarily any more open or that rates of social mobility (the extent to which individuals are able to move up or down the class structure) have increased. Indeed, evidence from the Sutton Trust (2005) would imply that such mobility as there was has decreased and that Britain and the U.S.A. remain less open than other societies.

Between the snobs and the yobs

In fact, towards the top end of the class structure, educational credentials continue to have less significance than other forms of cultural capital which are transmitted via family connections and through the network of private 'public' schools that have their own longstanding links with élite universities. Qualifications are therefore necessary but not sufficient 'to get a foot in the door' but not to get through it. Ultimately, for those at the very top, sometimes referred to as the upper or ruling class, or merely 'the élite', this type of cultural capital is supported by levels of wealth, property and financial capital unavailable to others lower down the occupational hierarchy.

Below the élite are what could previously have been defined as the 'established middle class' that some sociologists call 'the service class' of senior managers and higher professionals, who can also be seen as an 'upper middle' class. They rely on being able to secure entry to the more academic state schools in premium suburban areas. Or they have the financial resources to ensure that in the absence of a 'good' local school, private education secures their children's entry to one of the Russell Group of élite 'researching universities', or at least to one of the better 'teaching universities' (not—save for exceptional and specific courses—to 'training universities' with their links to further education). In this respect, it is no accident that in inner London, for example, where a 'gentrified' middle class lives next door to those still clinging to the remnants of social housing, 13 per cent of parents rely on the private school sector compared with nearly 8 per cent nationally. (The situation is replicated in other cities, such as Bristol which we mention in connection with private schooling discussed in chapter five.)

Meanwhile the majority of the population make up a new but also an increasingly fragmented 'working middle' of society where there has been a slight rise in those occupations that can be considered white-collar and above. These are up from some 35 per cent to 37 per cent of the total of directly employed and self-employed occupations in the UK labour market since 1992, according to successive Labour Force Surveys. The increase in computer managers, software engineers and programmers, as well as in self-employment, could be said to reflect some growth in the much touted 'knowledge economy.' These 'knowledge workers' join the 'Middle England' of 'hard working families' that is also ideologically presented as the norm by the popular press and politicians whose electoral bids are aimed at winning over this 'centre ground.'

The working-middle could be said also to include other areas of the economy where there has been real growth in services and sales, as well as in offices. Alongside this has been an expansion in support workers, especially in health and education services with increased work for carers such as care assistants, welfare and community workers and nursery nurses. These are often low paid jobs, many of them carried out by women. Meanwhile, the same statistical sources indicate manual workers still account for a relatively stable 10.5 million workers—approaching 40 per cent of total employment. If clerical and secretarial work is added to this then the traditional labour force stands at some 15 million—approaching two in three jobs. This belies the notion of a substantial shift in the demand for labour.

However, many in this majority group find that they invariably need to acquire more and more educational credentials both to obtain and keep (through perpetual training and retraining) stable/core employment and be guaranteed 'a proper job.' So gaining relatively high levels of qualifications continues to be essential if they are to maintain their position and avoid falling into the new so-called 'underclass' that has also been ideologically and politically constructed beneath them and into which illness, unemployment, accident or the lack of worthwhile qualifications could so easily cast them. This 'rough' section of the traditionally manually working class could be seen as a new version of Marx's 'lumpenproletariat', semi-employed, casualised and low-paid but also an increasingly prominent part of society, ducking and diving in peripheral 'McJobs' and including economic migrants legal and illegal from the EU and elsewhere. For some social commentators, like Castells (1996), the expansion of 'McJobs' is as significant as the growth of the professional and managerial sector noted above, while both Toynbee (2003) in the UK and Ehrenreich (2002) in the U.S.A. have provided detailed accounts of the life of 'the new poor.'

Children and young people identified—even before they are born—as belonging to this 'Status Zero' group are policed, curfewed, ASBO-ed, tagged and mentored by arbitrary and repressive state measures on the basis of their 'risk of social exclusion.' In schools they find themselves medicated, statemented and on correctional behavioural programmes in 'sin bins', if not excluded to Pupil Referral Units and/or under the supervision of Youth Offending Teams. As 'persistent truants', whose absence from school is unofficially tolerated, many still fall through the Careers Service net and they eventually disappear into the dodgy economy. For too many of them in the country with the highest prison population in Europe, as for their counterparts in the U.S.A, *Learning to Labor in New Times* is less a preparation for employment and independent living than for 'Learning to do time' (Nolan and Anyon 2004).

This permanent pool of un-and semi-employed maintains downward pressure on the wages of those in the hollowed out middle who live in fear and loathing of this derided and criminalised 'underclass' beneath them. The growth of ICT and services continues to erode the former manual-mental division of knowledge and labour between the post-war middle and working classes. Meanwhile, the pressure on companies to downsize and outsource work overseas further reduces core employment and increases insecurity and pressure on the majority working-middle of the population. Thus, as secure core employment contracts and work is contracted out to a growing insecure periphery, those in the new middle are caught 'between the snobs and the yobs'.

Jon Cruddas MP calls this an 'hour-glass economy'. In the top half of the hour glass there has been an increase in high paid jobs, performed by those with significant discretion over their hours and patterns of work. In a general sense they might be described as the 'knowledge workers' of the supposed 'knowledge economy' to which government effort is dedicated. However, in the UK, the growth at the bottom of the hour glass of low paid, unskilled and insecure, often part-time work in occupations prominent fifty years ago has been more significant. So much so that 'twenty years of schooling' may still result in working on the day shift, that is if the day shift continues to exist at all!

Social progress or social control?

In this book we want to emphasise the increased importance of education in the 'social control' of a generation of young people who, compared with their counterparts of fifty years ago, now experience a very different relationship to the labour market. In contrast to official wisdom about the positive challenge of globalisation for education and employment, we would argue that many of the developments in schools, colleges and universities, are, on the contrary, the result of the negative consequences of economic restructuring on the lives of young people.

With the breakdown of the traditional avenues of transition from school to work and the replacement of the manual/non-manual divide by an increasingly credentialised occupational structure, educational institutions are required to restore 'order' to the lives of young people. This is not to argue that social control has not previously been a significant function of education; only to maintain that because of the changes outlined above, the part played by schools and colleges in exercising social control has increased. As psychologists put it, 'the locus of control' has shifted with the decline of regular lifelong earning from wages at work towards Foundation Learning in extended schooling and Lifelong Learning thereafter. So that, instead of wages regulating legitimate access to the collective wealth of society and with many welfare benefits now conditional on work or training (workfare if not learningfare), it is with the promise of often receding eventual employment that society now placates its 'angry and defrauded young'.

This is particularly the case in relation to the education of minority ethnic students. Although, along with the overall average rise in results, each of the main ethnic groups now achieve higher attainments than ever before, as with all pupils, the gap between the highest and lowest achieving groups is widening even as overall attainment is rising. Although again, as Dave Gillborn and Hiedi Mirza caution, care should be taken that 'Emphasising difference in attainment between groups ... does not lead to a hierarchy of ethnic minorities based on assumptions of inherent ability'(2000, 38), the statistics demonstrate that 'between 1988 and 1997 ... Indian pupils ... moved from 23 per cent to 49 per cent' 5 GCSE A-Cs (above the all white average), while 'Bangla-Deshi pupils moved by 19 per cent over the same period' (ibid). As a result, not only Bangla-Deshi but 'African-Caribbean and Pakistani pupils [also] are markedly less likely to attain five higher grade GCSEs than their white, Chinese and Indian peers nationally'.

These groups, like the poorest of white pupils (see Evans, 2006), have drawn least benefit from the rising average levels of attainment and the gap between them and the average is bigger now than a decade ago. Moreover, attainment varies over time at school so that, as Gillborn and Mirza also show for African-Caribbean pupils particularly:

> 'Available evidence suggests that the inequalities of attainment become progressively greater as they move through the school system; such differences become more pronounced between the end of primary school and the end of secondary education.'   (ibid)

Nevertheless, Black African and African-Caribbean students are over-represented in further and higher education compared to their proportion in the age-range (giving the lie to the allegation that they and their parents are uninterested in education). Even so, their numbers are largest in the least prestigious institutions. London Metropolitan University, for example, has more black and minority ethnic students than the top twenty 'Russell Group' of élite universities put together.

In sum, although discrimination is no longer so crude as when Bernard Coard wrote *How the West Indian child is made educationally subnormal in the British school system* in 1971, despite the succession of assimilationist, multicultural but not anti-racist education policies, as Professor Gus John says,

'Throughout the last four decades education and schooling as well as that historical by-product of theirs, underachievement, have become increasingly racialised.'   (2005, 97)

The encouragement of 'Faith Schools', open only to the adherents of particular religions, against all the evidence of the accumulated bitterness of such segregated schooling in Northern Ireland, can only enhance this trend. The current 'debate' on multiculturalism typically ignores this contradiction as it proposes returning to colour-blind national assimilation instead of going forward to institutionalised anti-racism.

The persistent privatisation of 'post-comprehensive' education also constantly seeks to introduce new divisions between different learners in many different ways. In this it could be said to reflect wider processes of global neoliberalism. At the same time as this 'erases borders for speculation ... it multiplies borders for human beings', as subcommandante Marcos has noted. Consequently, he writes 'countries are obliged to erase their national borders ... but to multiply their internal borders.' As a result, 'neoliberalism doesn't turn many countries into one country; it turns each country into many countries', making 'racism a new religion.' Education is therefore just one instance of 'the violent supermarket that neoliberalism is selling us' in which 'global decomposition is taking place.'

Identical processes of commodification that quantify provision packaged at different prices for various niche markets can be seen in other former-welfare state services, such as housing and health. In the former, at one pole gated communities close themselves off and, at the other, 'sink estates' are closed off from the rest of society. In the latter, private health insurance buys private care as the remainder of the former-National Health Service sinks towards a residual 'safety net' subsisting on charity.

Personalised learning

New Labour politicians disclaim any elements of selectivity in their approach of equitably treating all pupils, students and trainees individually but not equally. In particular, they deny similarities between their present policies and the 1944 Act, promising 'no return to selection.' Yet current learning policies introduce subtle new forms of selection at every level. They reach down even into infant schools with batteries of tests that start at earlier ages as teachers are encouraged to differentiate between HAPs, MAPs and LAPs (higher, middle and lower achieving pupils). These are 'the gifted and talented, the just plain average and the struggling' as the 2005 White Paper unsubtly distinguished them (p. 20).

Different 'learning styles' supposedly disguise and justify these differences while pupils diagnosed with new forms of learning difficulties and disabilities are often medicalised for drug treatment. This is despite the rejection of the medical model, according to which some children are 'normal' and others 'handicapped', by the Warnock committee whose conclusions formed the basis of the 1981 Education Act. In a further extension of the comprehensive ideal, this gave the right for all children to be included in mainstream schools, provided they did not adversely affect the learning of others. Now that so many special schools have been closed and their children included but often not adequately supported in mainstream schools, Baroness Warnock argues that this has been 'carried too far' (2005). The government's answer to this as to other special needs, including those of the 'gifted and talented', is the 'personalised' learning which is so heavily featured in the 2005 White Paper.

'Personalised' learning, echoing the 'personalised instruction' of behaviourist psychology, is the latest perversion of the comprehensive ideal that promises to treat every pupil individually so as not to be seen to fail the many while selecting the few. For it is clear that the promotion of personalised learning is concerned to identify specific types of learning for particular groups of students. This would seem to contradict the arguments rehearsed above about the increasingly generic demands of the new economy requiring flexible employees to train and retrain lifelong for a succession of new and demanding occupations in a globally competitive economy.

It is indeed absurdly contradictory for the government to encourage young people to pursue narrow vocational specialisms from 14-years-old with secondary schools designated as specialist business, sports, retail or IT academies and to reject the proposals of Sir Mike Tomlinson's working group on A-level reform that represented a step, albeit a very small one, towards closing the gap between vocational and academic learning. Yet, rather than exploiting opportunities for creating a comprehensive post-16 education as the first stage of genuine lifelong learning, New Labour's 2005 *14-19* White Paper intensified these divisions, creating a system of 'different horses for different courses' and the emergence of a new form of 21st century tripartism.

Meanwhile private schooling remains untouched by any of these 'vocational' developments to allow access for those who can afford it through traditional academic qualifications to élite universities. With the introduction and raising of student fees, likely to rise again soon towards full cost (currently averaging over £18,000 a year for undergraduate tuition at Oxford), these are also becoming prohibitive save for the wealthiest students. This is especially the case for longer and more expensive courses, such as medicine and postgraduate study. The link between cultural capital enabling 'effortless achievement' by those from privileged backgrounds and the real money capital of those who will soon be the only ones able to afford acquiring it in the private and 'better'/semi-privatised and most selective state schools will thus be rendered transparent. It will not be disguised by the university access regulator (nicknamed OffToff), nor by the encouragement of US-style bursaries that no English universities can afford.

Nevertheless, the former Education Secretary Charles Clarke stated:

> 'Demand for graduates is very strong, and research shows that 80 per cent of the 1.7 million new jobs which are expected to be created by the end of the decade will be in occupations which normally recruit those with higher education qualifications.'

As Cruddas who quotes this comments,

> 'Clarke ignores the fact that a high proportion of this relates to NVQ Level 3 and not higher education qualifications. Once this extra growth is taken out then the figure for new jobs by 2010 requiring a degree drops to 55 per cent.'

Most jobs that are advertised are not of course new jobs but seek to replace an employee who has left so that:

> 'Overall, when the government's own statistics are broken down they actually reveal that by 2010 the figure for those in employment required to be first degree graduates or postgraduates will be 22.1 per cent—or 77.9 per cent of jobs will not require a degree.'

Cruddas sees this as further evidence for 'an ever clearer polarisation within the labour market' and an 'hour-glass economy' (above):

> 'On the one hand, a primary labour market—or the knowledge-based economy—covering about 21 per cent of jobs. On the other hand

an expanding secondary labour market where the largest growth is occurring—in service-related elementary occupations, administrative and clerical occupations, sales occupations, caring personal service occupations and the like.'

Vocational training for some while widening participation for others

In state schools the experience of vocational education during the last decade not only provides another salient example of the lack of correspondence between education and the economy but of the growing role of education and training in social control. Originally based on notions of 'occupational competence' and designed as a challenge to traditional qualifications, vocational qualifications like the General National Vocational Qualification (GNVQ) have 'drifted' to resemble the academic qualifications their creators were so critical of. Rather than facilitating entry to employment, Advanced level GNVQs (or Vocational/Applied A-levels as they are now called) have been used more as an alternative route into higher education by students, particularly those applying to the post-1992 universities.

Teachers and lecturers have both welcomed and encouraged the increased participation in higher education. However, it has meant increasing numbers of young people having a very narrow and vocationally specific experience of education and has led to accusations of so-called 'dumbing down.' The contradictions behind the official dedication to vocational education and simultaneous commitment to academic standards is the subject of further discussion in the chapters that follow.

The policy of widening participation to higher education, which we also examine, is plainly contradicted by the simultaneous raising of student fees. This makes the 2010 target for half of 18-30 year-olds to experience some form of higher education unattainable but it has also had the effect of squeezing over 30-year-olds out of universities. The lack of funding for anyone else is also a cause of the crisis in adult education where many colleges and institutes have closed and more are threatened with closure. Nor are most people 30-plus willing to take out loans for full fees to go to university even on the never-never. Since the introduction of up-front fees for all UK higher education in 1997, they have fallen as a proportion of all undergraduates. The further rise in English university fees in 2006 reduced applications from them again, along with traditionally working-class and many minority ethnic applicants, so that total student numbers dropped by 15,000 according to the admissions service, UCAS.

This was predicted by everyone except the government since the aspiration to widen participation is so obviously contradicted by fees. It has not been helped by most Vice Chancellors pitching their fees at £3000 in the pretence that if they all charge the same there is no market so business will continue as usual whilst they make up for previous shortfalls with the maximum currently allowed. Yet, in what the government clearly regards as an interim and experimental period before the £3,000 cap comes off, some universities are advertising the currently available grants and loans as a strategy to attract low income students, as well as offering local further education and sixth-form students lower entry grades, tying working-class students to local universities.

However, most universities compete on bursaries and bribes—free lap tops and IPods—while the élite give scholarships to the most academic applicants at the same time enhancing their traditional 'excellence' for those who can afford to pay what will soon be de-capped fees. A race to the bottom may result for the teaching and training universities, further reducing their entry requirements along with fees. Just like Australia which introduced similar student fees in 1994, as overall fees rise so does student debt while applications and entry requirements fall and institutions merge or close.

All this turns large parts of higher education into further education while widening participation is presented as a professionalisation of the proletariat that masks the actual proletarianisation of the professions, not least the academic profession. Even amongst the élite Russell Group of researching universities, this Americanised system in which many more have degrees tends towards 'real higher education' starting at even more expensive post-graduate school. In the competition that can be anticipated from the free market in fees, only those universities with such schools—especially Medical Schools—can expect to survive.

Education Minister Alan Johnson finally dropped the fifty per cent target in summer 2006. But even if it could have been reached as originally intended by 2010, this would still leave the question first raised by the 1963 Newsom Report on secondary modern schools: what about the more than *Half Our Future* who do not progress to mass higher education. The same question faces the schools that may be incorporated by the 2006 Education Act which lose out in the competition for sixth forms. The implications of these changes for the survival and revival of the progressive comprehensive education advanced in the 1960s and 1970s will be discussed later in this book.

Conclusion

This opening chapter has sought to provide the context for understanding developments in education policy over the last 20 years and more. It has challenged the official orthodoxy on the relationship between education and economic performance and discussed how changes in the occupational structure and the recomposition of class have given education a new role in social control as the age of entry into the labour market has been raised for all but a minority. If at the official level of political rhetoric, education continues to be presented as a potential leveller, it is, we would argue, increasingly functioning to divide learners at all levels from one another.

Divisions between pupils and students within schools, colleges and universities have been combined with the increasing diversity of institutions which, while officially promoting more 'choice' for some, has resulted in the emergence of a tiered system of provision in all sectors. Infant and primary schools prepare pupils for selection by specialist secondaries following either academic, vocational, or basic skills pathways. Similarly at further education, there are tertiary grammars (Sixth Form Colleges), technicals (Centres of Vocational Excellence), and moderns (General Further Education Colleges). While in higher education, Charles Clarke presented a Platonic Holy Trinity of

> 'the great research universities, the outstanding teaching universities and those that make a dynamic, dramatic contribution to their regional and local economies'

in reply to his first Parliamentary question as Secretary of State for Education reported in *The Times Higher*, 6 December 2002.

The chapters that follow chart what has gone wrong in England's schools, colleges and universities in terms of the wider contradictions indicated above.

Chapter 2

What was ever right with English education? 1944 and all that

This chapter examines in more detail the period of educational expansion that followed the passing of the 1944 Education Act. It describes how this expansion both reflected and supported the economic recovery of the post-war years but also how it incorporated rather than challenged many of the historical inequities and 'peculiarities' that have long been a feature of English society. It sees the growth of the comprehensive education movement as part of general advances in education from primary to postgraduate level in the 1960s and 1970s. But it also discusses how, as the period of post-war economic prosperity came to an end, the Labour Party, the political Party most associated both with educational expansion and with promoting comprehensive and other progressive ideas, came to implement policies that paved the way for dismantling comprehensive education along with the rest of the welfare state by Conservative and New Labour governments in the years that followed.

The peculiarities of the English

The passing of the 1944 Education Act was part of a general social and economic reconstruction and 'modernisation' of society after the Second World War. Until the Act, Britain was unique amongst industrialised countries in not having an education system that matched its economic progress. Despite pioneering industrial revolution to become 'the workshop of the world' in the nineteenth century, compared with many of its European competitors and the U.S.A., England's education system was woefully underdeveloped. It was also remarkably parochial and for a long time dependent on the contribution of voluntary and religious organisations. In fact, England had no public education as such until 1870 and it was not free for all until 1892.

England thus lagged far behind France and the U.S.A. which established a republican entitlement to free public education with their revolutions. Meanwhile in Germany and elsewhere the state sponsored national schooling together with industrial training to a high technical level. Instead, the Manchester school of economists in England emphasised pursuing economic self-interest rather than collective cooperation. They advocated a 'minimalist' state which restricted itself, as far as it possibly could, to maintaining law and order and national defence.

Though the need for increases in the levels of workplace skills became an important factor, the expansion of state education was driven as much by political necessity as economic expediency. Indeed, the efforts of Robert Owen and other reformers to get working-class children into schools had to compete with early industrial capitalism's insatiable appetite for child labour. The expansion of public education was bound up with the extension of the suffrage, particularly the realisation that if the lower orders were not sufficiently educated by their superiors, then there was always the very real danger that they would want to educate themselves! In this respect, it was no accident that extensions of mass schooling often coincided with periods of political and economic militancy amongst the working class.

Italian Marxist Antonio Gramsci coined the term 'hegemony' to describe the particular significance of the ideological as opposed to the economic power of the ruling class. The argument of this chapter, indeed a major theme of the book, is that the gradual extension of mass state education from 1870 onwards should be seen as an hegemonic exercise. It was a response to the need for class control, as much as a process of developing specific workplace skills, let alone beneficent enlightenment. For Gramsci, achieving hegemony was about winning 'consent.' But exercising hegemony or winning 'legitimacy' did not mean that the working classes would have to be persuaded by taught propaganda to endorse the values of the ruling class; more that they were not able to develop coherent ideas to oppose them. It might also require the granting of short-term concessions to ensure the longer term stability of ruling-class interests.

Thus, the 1944 Education Act has been widely described as a 'compromise' or 'settlement' between different interest groups and social classes. As an integral part of post-war social reconstruction, it was an expression of a wide ranging commitment to a fairer society. At the same time, it preserved gross inequality, chiefly between classes but also between the genders, those of different abilities and, later, ethnicity. In this situation, an emphasis on 'equal opportunities' and 'meritocracy', for everyone to have equal access to success, was vital to gaining legitimacy for the new system of schooling.

The limitations of the 1944 settlement

Compared to what had been on offer before, the 1944 Act was certainly a great step forward and was endorsed by the Labour and trade union movement. But, as with other post-war social reforms, its scope was limited. Being primarily a 'catching up' exercise, it introduced measures established in other industrialised countries a century earlier, while, in accommodating major parts of the existing social order, it did not fundamentally alter the relationships between class and education.

The most significant feature of the 1944 Act, for example, was the way in which it accepted existing assumptions about the occupational order. The creators of the three different types of secondary school argued that they catered for different levels of ability which could be 'scientifically' distinguished by the 11-plus 'IQ' test. This was disputed by the new sociological research of the 1950s that grew up in response to the introduction of mass secondary schooling, especially at the London School of Economics. It quickly identified a 'waste of talent' in those rejected by the system as congenitally uneducable to higher levels. It also exposed the difficulties experienced by many of the few working-class children who did reach the grammar school.

For the majority failed by the 11-plus, the Victorian 'apprentice boy' model of early school leaving that had developed with the industrial revolution persisted unchanged. Heavy industry was reconstructed along historical lines and not modernised after the war, as it was elsewhere in Europe. Most girls too left school as soon as possible to marry young, encouraged by William Beveridge, the founder of the welfare state, 'to replenish the stock of the race.' The 'compromise' or 'settlement' between employers and unions, representing 'the two sides of industry', guaranteed full employment for men—lifelong earning from 15-65—and paid them 'a family wage' on which to support children and a wife who worked part-time if at all.

Rather than the 'Lifelong Learning' which was later to become a slogan, most children left school as soon as possible. Even for those few who were selected to stay on, their education was 'front loaded.' It ended when they matriculated at 18, or—exceptionally—after taking their 'final degree' at 21. Only a very small crew of academics went further. Although it had enjoyed some spectacular successes, research and its technological application was limited. Industrial apprenticeship was also age restricted by definition.

The new sociological studies soon established the correlation between a father's employment and a boy's educational destiny. Far from promoting classlessness and equal opportunities, the tripartite secondary school system served to limit working-class mobility into the middle class. The chances for most working-class children remained slim, although in some places—South Wales for example—the number of grammar schools was much higher. According to Floud et al. (1956), on average the son of a 'skilled manual' father had a 14-18 per cent chance of making it to grammar school, compared with the 60 per cent chance of the son of a professional/managerial father.

So, if the 1944 Act denied the middle class the chance to buy a place at grammar if not private school, as those who could afford it had previously been able to do, it was clear that with an unreformed academic curriculum they were able to enjoy instead the advantages of what later became referred to as 'cultural capital.' This was the middle-class ethos of the home with its resources of books and access to 'high culture' which reinforced that of the school. By comparison, while there were clear advantages for working-class children who passed the 11-plus and entered grammar school, there were also, as Jackson and Marsden (1962) vividly described, many cultural barriers to contend with once there. Moreover, most of those who stayed the course against the odds could then bid *Goodbye to the Working Class* (Greenslade 1976). The system was self-perpetuating.

The 1944 Act was not therefore a step towards the classless society to which many aspired after the war but there were other significant historical legacies which the Act accepted rather than sought to confront. To begin with, educational planning remained at a local level. Although since the 1902 Act, power of provision had transferred from elected school boards to Local Education Authorities, there was little in the way of any national plan. LEAs were free to interpret many of the decisions of central government in ways they felt were appropriate. The Ministry had little clout—especially compared with today—and the position of Minister of Education did not merit full Cabinet rank and could usually be left to a woman.

In addition, the Anglican and Catholic churches continued to be responsible for large numbers of both primary and secondary schools. Now included in the LEA system, they enjoyed the advantages of public funding in exchange for the minor concession of LEA representation on their governing bodies. Thus, they continued to perpetuate religious prejudice throughout their curriculum with sectarian consequences in Northern Ireland, Scotland and elsewhere. Class and ethnic differences were also sustained in England, especially in relation to the largest minority Irish population.

Finally and most importantly, the Act left private education untouched. In fact, the influence of private education was strengthened by the formalisation of the direct grant grammar schools that received public funding in exchange for continuing to offer scholarships to local children. Meanwhile, the English 'public schools' continued to enjoy their cultural leadership within education, providing a model for all self-respecting grammar schools. So in terms of the curriculum, the teaching of Latin and the classics remained essential, but also in terms of a more general ethos that grammar schools mimicked. In cahoots with the antique universities via the exam boards, the 'great public schools' effectively dictated the academic curriculum that was followed by the grammar and other schools that sought to emulate them.

Oxford and Cambridge represented and sustained the peculiar English principle of selectivity on the basis of supposed inherited quality. This was the presupposition of the 11-plus 'IQ' test, later shown to be without any of the scientific foundation it claimed after a scandal revealed fiddled figures (see Chitty 2004b). But it was also the basis of the traditional university discrimination going back to Plato between 'Men of Gold, Silver and Bronze', or 'first, second and third class minds.' Instead of an entitlement to learning, this principle turns education into an obstacle race in which the majority fall at every fence. As a result, as Tim Brighouse quips: 'No matter how far you go in the English education system, they'll fail you in the end!' As we argue, this is still the case today—only more so.

Comprehensive struggles

It was against this background that the comprehensive movement emerged. The moves towards a more egalitarian secondary schooling were supported by a growing consensus across the political spectrum. This accepted that in an expanding economy, all young people, rather than just those who made up the grammar school minority, needed to be educated to much higher levels. The occupational structure was changing. Not only was it argued that blue-collar manual workers needed to be educated for more demanding employment, it was also the case that white-collar professional and service work was expanding.

However, though economic changes were important and education spending increased from three per cent to over six per cent of gross national product between 1951 and 1975, the comprehensive movement was spearheaded by powerful lobbying. Without this, change may not have taken place at all. As Caroline Benn and Clyde Chitty documented extensively at the time and later, the changes were as much 'bottom up' as they were 'top down.' 1963 was a high water mark, as Manchester and Liverpool—then much more influential industrial cities than they are today—went comprehensive supported by strong local campaigns.

'Top down' endorsement came two years later with the Labour government's 'request' that other councils do likewise. Seconded by the National Union of Teachers, popular support for comprehensives remained strong through the period of Conservative government between 1970-74. Ironically, the then-Secretary of State for Education, Margaret Thatcher, designated more comprehensive schools than any previous Education minister. The movement had become 'an unstoppable bandwagon', as she later complained in her Memoirs.

But the move towards comprehensives was by no means universal although it was supported by a committed network of activists who made up the 'comprehensive movement.' Reform was hindered by the fact that, despite being returned to office in 1964 with a clear policy of support for comprehensives, Labour did not attempt to legislate. Instead, DES Circular 10/65 merely 'requested' that local authorities submit plans for reform. This and the absence of any national agency for coordinating the break with selection, meant that the development of comprehensive schools would be relatively gradual, but also uneven and ad-hoc. Compared with the incentives given to creating 'grant maintained' schools in the 1990s for example, no extra money was available to speed the transition.

Reviewing the general progress of the move to comprehensives *Thirty years on* in 1996, Benn and Chitty reported that, whereas in Scotland and Wales 99 per cent of pupils were in schools calling themselves comprehensive, in England the figure was only 82.9 per cent, up from 8.5 per cent in 1965 (p. 88). Some LEAs have to this day refused to part with their grammar schools. In Kent and Buckinghamshire for example, the '11-plus' continues to haunt the lives of year six pupils, more even than the second round of SATs. Invariably, in such places as the London Borough of Kingston Upon Thames, schools not designated as grammars call themselves comprehensive, some even having sixth forms, but in the eyes of many parents remain 'secondary modern.'

At a more general level, even though a large majority of comprehensive schools were co-educational (according to Benn and Chitty's 1994 survey—94 per cent, p118), single-sex comprehensives—if this is not a contradiction in terms—continued to be significant. Separate schools for boys and girls were also likely to have voluntary aided (religious) status, perpetuating divisions between faiths and races as well as between genders.

It was the primary schools that came closest to achieving the comprehensive goal of inclusive schooling. They were the most likely to accept all who applied in their locality (although see further on school segregation by housing). Without having any longer to stream pupils in preparation for the 11-plus and before SATs performed the same divisive function, primary teachers were able to innovate unhampered by any requirements of an academic National Curriculum. They were encouraged by the 1967 Plowden Report which emphasised a child-centred, less formal approach to learning as well as emphasising the individual development of children. It is not coincidental that even today primary schools retain the closest loyalty and support of parents as opposed to secondaries, let alone further and higher education.

Streaming, setting or mixed ability?

If there were a variety of obstacles to comprehensive expansion, there was no consensus about how, once they had been set up, comprehensive schools should be internally organised. Right-wing critics of mixed-ability teaching for example, were (and still are) often ignorant of the fact that a majority of comprehensives, if not streaming their students in all subjects, continued to 'set' them for many subjects. According to Benn and Chitty, complete mixed-ability teaching where it occurred was largely confined to initial years. Only 80 of the 1, 230 schools in their survey used it in all subjects and in all years, a third of the sample having at least two subjects set and nearly a quarter having four.

A general move towards mixed ability teaching was hardly encouraged by the fact that comprehensive schools inherited not only an antiquated but also an élitist curriculum. In effect, the old grammar/public school academic curriculum was now extended to all who took public exams. Comprehensive secondaries were faced with established ideas about the importance of examination in a narrowly subject-based curriculum linked to GCE O-levels and A-levels. Until comparatively recently, these last were only taken by a small minority of the students as preparation for university entrance. Comprehensives therefore were under pressure to show that they could rival the academic achievement of the grammar schools. As a result, the need to emphasise the examination success of the few contradicted dealing with the inequalities faced by the many. The peculiarly English selectivity principle trumped the comprehensive principle of entitlement to equal opportunities.

But there were ways in which comprehensives aspired to challenge curriculum orthodoxy. The 1970s and early 1980s have been associated with what has become referred to as 'progressive education' (Jones, 1983). During these years a plethora of initiatives emerged, for example the Schools Council Humanities and the Nuffield Science projects. Centrally supported by the Schools Council and locally by LEA advisors and inspectors, additional funding was available for schools in Educational Priority Areas linked to Community Development Programmes of housing redevelopment and reorganised social services. The intention was to compensate for school catchment areas segregated by housing type. Large LEAs like Inner London also balanced their comprehensive intakes to ensure a social spread. Massive housing redevelopments with new schools were also undertaken, including efforts to build mixed class communities in new towns.

Anything seemed possible when, as Lady Plowden wrote in Volume 2 of her Report on primary education (p. 69):

'Unemployment has been almost non-existent since the war ... incomes have risen, nutrition has improved, housing is better, the health services and the rest of the social services have brought help where it is needed.'

In this optimistic atmosphere and in some inner city schools in particular, what could be seen as a 'soft progressivism' was accompanied by a more radical practice, particularly around English and the humanities which sought engagement with a burgeoning popular culture. More radical still were journals like *Teaching London Kids* which challenged not only knowledge and subject hierarchies, but also the structures of schools themselves.

Such initiatives were supported by the emergence of a 'new sociology of education.' This developed in some of the university education departments created from the old teacher training trade colleges that established teaching as a degree-entry, better-paid profession for the first time. The new approach made a radical critique of the school curriculum and explored the 'politics' of school knowledge, encouraging both would-be and existing teachers to question how the curriculum was constructed, in whose interests and for what purpose (Young 1971).

Such critiques coincided with attempts to move away from what was later called Eurocentrism towards international perspectives on history, geography, social studies and other subjects. Even as the first of a series of immigration acts from 1963 ended the period of post-war immigration from the former-imperial New Commonwealth, black and other minority ethnic groups battled against relegation to inferior schooling, indiscriminate bussing and for their own supplementary schools with recognition of minority languages and cultures in the curriculum. In response, the official pretence of 'colour-blind' assimilation gave way to recognition of the reality of multiculturalism if not to anti-racist education.

Even if, compared with the success of Plowden in primary education, the majority of secondary schools were not won over to the radical pedagogy of progressive education, its influence should not be discounted. If it was not able to seriously challenge traditional 'academic' approaches, it did establish itself in some of the new Mode 3 CSE courses set up as alternatives to them, particularly in English, social studies and humanities. A further analysis of the strengths and limitations of 1970s progressivism is included in chapter six.

Going higher and further

Mandatory awards from LEAs to meet costs of living plus tuition fees for full-time higher education students had already been introduced in 1962 when the 1963 Robbins Report rejected the idea that there was only a limited 'pool of ability' genetically able to benefit from higher education. Instead, Robbins established the principle that 'courses in higher education should be available for all those who are qualified by ability and attainment to pursue them and wish to do so.' This still left selection in the hands of academics, rather than establishing an entitlement to higher education, such as in France or Italy where students who graduate from high school can expect to enter their local university as of right. But it led to a rapid expansion of higher education with new purpose-built universities as well as upgraded technical ones. The new ones were set up largely in the image of the old as arts and humanities institutions.

Some of the new universities, such as Essex, were at the forefront of the student movement that was a worldwide consequence of higher education expansion to contain the demographic boom at the end of a period of sustained prosperity. This expansion coincided with new ideas from decolonisation abroad and rising popular demands at home and, linked to these, the development of a 'new left.' In the UK 'student unrest' was, as much as anything else, a product of the frustrated expectations of a generation of students, the majority of whose parents had not attended higher education and for whom promises of access to new and more demanding job opportunities were unlikely to be met. Many of 'the graduates of 68' carried their idealism into teaching at all levels.

The growth of the universities was supplemented not only by the Open University but by the sudden announcement in 1965 of another new type of higher education with 30 polytechnics under the control of Local Education Authorities. This 'binary policy' was urged upon the government by DES officials alarmed at the cost of the university expansion proposed by Robbins. They sought to protect the smaller and better funded 40 odd independently existing antique, Victorian civic or 'redbrick' and new universities from the pressure to change exerted by increasing student numbers.

Polys were supposed to benefit local students following more vocational, technical and less academic courses related to their local labour markets. Even though Anthony Crosland, the Labour Education Minister, said that he 'did not want any rigid dividing line between the different sectors—quite the contrary', the 'binary line' he now created between the new polytechnics and the already existing and new universities institutionally polarised higher education. It generated and sustained—in this sector of education as elsewhere—an opposition between academicism and vocationalism, or education against training. So selection was moved up the age range to tertiary level just as it was being phased out at secondary level through comprehensive schools.

Despite this, many of those involved in establishing the new polytechnics advocated 'higher education for all.' This would for the first time offer 'careers for all', instead of interesting careers in the professions for the few and dull, repetitive and dead-end jobs for the many. Seen as 'the people's universities' (in the Fabian socialist Sidney Webb's phrase) by some of their idealistic founders, the polytechnics aimed to foster what was called a liberal vocationalism. This paralleled simultaneous developments in the comprehensive and community schools that were not wholly given over to the academic ideal. Like comprehensive schools, polytechnics aimed to make available for students studying locally 'equal opportunities' to qualify for occupations on equal terms with those educated selectively. Thus, one of their founders, Eric Robinson, saw the new institutions creating 'a bridgehead' for a 'comprehensive system of education for adults', replacing 'the concept of the boarding school university by that of the urban community university' (1968, 34).

Still, polytechnic expansion was insufficient to meet the growing demand for higher education. Further Education took up the slack at the same time as the traditional industrial apprenticeships it had catered for began to wane. Further education and adult education pioneered access to higher education, together with some progressive extra mural (sic) departments at traditional universities. They offered a second chance for qualification to those failed by academic schooling.

Technical education, which government had not been prepared to fund in the technical secondary schools after the war, had already migrated to further education. Section 41 of the 1944 Education Act had required LEAs to provide 'adequate facilities' for further and adult education defined as 'full-or part-time education for those over school age' and 'leisure, cultural and recreational activities for those willing and able to benefit from them.'

The colleges also responded to demand for and from growing numbers of young women who began to attend courses that prepared them for work in the expanding office and service sectors of employment. Further education, adult education and 'outreach' from higher education pioneered access for adults to university at one end of provision, while further education colleges also built links with special schools to take often severely disabled people out of long-stay hospitals at the other. Typically, further education developed as the key area of education supporting growth in the economy with the skills people needed for employment.

Yet further education was associated with the trades rather than the professions and therefore with the traditional manually working rather than the non-manual middle class. However, it aimed to be open to all and from the 1970s onwards, as governments of both Parties attempted to control and reduce public expenditure, this led in some places to the establishment of tertiary colleges. These became the sole provider of courses of all kinds to all those over the age of 16 living in a particular area. The 1981 Macfarlane Report recommended that, for educational and costs reasons, tertiary colleges should be adopted as official policy but this was rejected by Mrs. Thatcher. This represented a lost moment for further education which from then on was left in competition for younger students with school sixth forms.

The process of going tertiary had begun with Exeter in 1970. As Caroline Benn and Clyde Chitty pointed out (1996), tertiary colleges were created to promote the development of comprehensive education not merely to rationalise A-level teaching (like the sixth-form colleges and centres) or offer a limited range of work-related qualifications (like many further education colleges still). Conservative-controlled authorities sometimes led the way since many were in mainly rural areas with small sixth forms and under-used colleges. By 1992 there were 57 tertiary colleges with 90,000 full-time 16-19 year-old students.

There was, though, less possibility of such tertiary reorganisation in the large Labour-controlled cities. Partly this was because some parents and most school teachers fought to preserve their sixth forms. Partly it was because many Labour councillors, who were committed to comprehensives, thought of these as 11-18 schools with sixth forms, like grammar schools. Even in large Northern cities, like Sheffield and Manchester, where Labour Councils reorganised provision at 16-plus, the move to a tertiary system was incomplete. Some schools retained their sixth forms, later threatening to opt-out if they were not allowed to keep them. The opportunity was thus lost to bring further education into the mainstream state education system by carrying forward the comprehensive reform of secondary schooling to a tertiary level. This would have normalised the transition from school at 16 to full-or part-time attendance at college by all school-leavers until a US-style graduation to full citizenship at 18. In addition, many adults were already at their local further education/tertiary college full-or part-time where they have always been the majority of students.

Hard times: the Black Papers and the 'Great Debate'

From the second half of the 1970s with the end of the 'long boom' that had sustained full employment since the war there was a consequent reduction of opportunities especially for school leavers. Governments therefore began to intervene more closely in the content and organisation of education and training. The emphasis given to opening up educational opportunities through comprehensives and expanded further and higher education was replaced with one that tried to reassert the link between schooling and social control.

Opposition to comprehensive education continued to be fuelled by the right-wing press. During the 1970s, this opposition was expressed most emphatically by the notorious Black Papers. The authors, who included novelist Kingsley Amis and the high profile London headteacher, Rhodes Boyson, who later became a Tory junior minister under Mrs. Thatcher, set out to engineer a public outcry about education. Initially they opposed the university expansion recommended by Robbins with Amis's slogan 'more means worse.' The Black Paperites were particularly agitated by 'revolting students' at the London School of Economics and elsewhere.

They then went on to attack both progressive pedagogy and Plowden for 'lowering standards' in primary schools. They defended the grammar school tradition and called for a return to discipline in schools where pupils were demonstrating against uniforms and corporal punishment. They advocated privileged 'excellence' and 'freedom' against what they saw as a generation of state levellers and called for more control over teachers. Increasingly, they fixated on 'race' and the threat of immigration to 'traditional British values.'

There is no evidence of any direct influence of the Black Papers over Labour education policy. However, in launching the 'Great Debate' on education in a speech at Ruskin College, Oxford in October 1976, Labour Prime Minister James Callaghan responded to their demands by calling for greater control over not only what was learnt but also over how it was organised. A key subtext of Callaghan's speech was that since government had lost control of the economy, it could at least assert its control over education with a new emphasis on vocationalism. 'Counter-cyclical training' would prepare school leavers for work once the economy picked up again. Meanwhile, instead of humanistic education for its own sake, study in schools should cultivate the 'realistic' attitudes to work that were allegedly being lost through progressive teaching. Echoing corporate capitalists and their supporters in the populist press in absurdly blaming schools and teachers for creating unemployment, Callaghan announced the termination of Old Labour's comprehensive project claiming that it was now complete or had indeed gone too far.

Callaghan's speech should also be seen as an introductory chapter to a political programme that has sought to reorganise not just schools, but also colleges and universities around a different set of objectives. This has been a long term project, carried out by Thatcherite Conservative and New Labour governments in different ways, but essentially with the same aim, the reassertion of the significance of education as a form of social control rather than as a vehicle for promoting equal opportunities and social justice. Part of this project has been to challenge the assumption that education should always be provided through the public sector as opposed to the market place. Before the arrival of Mrs. Thatcher in 1979, Old Labour began to put some of these foundation stones in place.

Harder times still: Training without jobs

A major consequence of economic downturn in the 1970s was that youth unemployment rocketed. Because of the disappearance of many of the jobs that school leavers habitually entered and, in particular, the winding down of apprenticeships, young people were to suffer more than any other sector of the working population. By 1975, the rate of unemployment, which during the 1950s and 1960s had averaged about 1.5 per cent (mainly in the 'depressed regions'), more than doubled so that it rose over half a million under Heath's government with 1.3 million being out of work by 1977. Whereas total unemployment increased by 45 per cent between 1972 and 1977, for those under-20 it increased by 120 per cent.

A result of this was the arrival and predominance of a new educational 'partner'—the Manpower Services Commission. The MSC was set up in 1974 on the quasi-autonomous non-governmental agency or 'quango' model intended by Heath to bring private sector entrepreneurialism into the civil service. Despite being officially accountable to the Secretary of State for Employment, the MSC was allowed to intervene directly in both further education and training as well as in the labour market. From 1977 the MSC's Youth Opportunities Programme (YOP) offered places for 250,000 unemployed 16-18 year-olds. Programmes varied from two week induction schemes through to three month training sessions or six months work experience with an employer. By 1982, with a Conservative government that allowed official unemployment to rise to an unprecedented three and a half million, half a million school leavers were signed up for YOPs.

MSC rhetoric emphasised the changing needs of employers. New workers, it was decreed, needed much greater 'flexibility' with a much wider skills repertoire. In educational terms this meant emphasising so-called 'transferable' competencies and new aptitudes and attitudes. MSC courses were designed to instil these. Given a progressive twist that appropriated the critique previously made of traditional academicism, the 'new vocationalism', as it became known by both converts and critics, pointed to the failure of education and by association, teachers and lecturers, to develop the qualities needed for employment.

The nearly two thirds of school leavers who entered the Youth Training Scheme (YTS) by the end of the 1980s were, therefore, provided with 'social and life skills' courses to compensate for the inadequacies they had acquired at school. Employers benefited financially from displacing regular employees with subsidised trainees they let go at the end of their year or two years 'training', so they supported MSC schemes. But the MSC was also supported by the Trades Union Congress, misled by the promise of a national apprenticeship system on a German 'social partnership' model.

The MSC was not abolished for all its 'interference' in the labour market by the incoming Conservative administration as Mrs. Thatcher had promised before the election. Instead, after the inner city 'riots' or 'Uprisings' of 1981, the Ministry of Social Control as it was widely known became a central part of her authoritarian social agenda. According to Finn (1987), YOPs and its successor, the YTS, represented a new direction in education policy. In response to rising youth unemployment, the Tories not only expanded YTS, they also made participation compulsory, despite the largest ever UK-wide school student strike against this in 1985.

Conservative politicians such as Lord Young, the Chairman of the MSC, aspired to extend the influence of the quango into the school sector. The 1982 Technical and Vocational Initiative (TVEI), for instance, was designed—in the first instance at least—to create a technical stream within comprehensive schools as an alternative to the academic route in the upper years of secondary school. As Sir Keith Joseph, Mrs. Thatcher's mentor as well as her Education Minister, said, if he could not reintroduce differences between state secondary schools by bringing back grammars, he would introduce differences within comprehensive schools. However, teachers and lecturers in schools and colleges were then still strong enough to subvert TVEI and make it compatible with comprehensive principles (see chapter six for a more detailed assessment).

In the run up to the third Conservative election victory in 1987, spending on the MSC reached record levels as its schemes and programmes were used to disguise what was now widely accepted by economists as permanent and structural unemployment. However, the economy began to recover temporarily from the severe recession the Tories had aggravated through their pursuit of monetarist economics (when between 1980 and 1983 one third of British manufacturing jobs disappeared). Responsibility for 'industrial training' was then handed over to local employer-dominated Training and Enterprise Councils (TECs). The balance of power in the Conservative Party was shifting away from 'modernisers' like Young and back to those who wanted a more traditional approach to education. After all the 'impossible to estimate' (Young) billions that had been spent on it, TVEI lost out to the academic ten subject National Curriculum that was introduced as part of the 'Great' Education Reform Act in 1988.

Meanwhile school leavers were voting with their feet, preferring to remain in the 'new school sixth forms' or go to further education college and then higher education rather than join 'dead-end schemes'. They were able to qualify for continued learning due to the boost which had been given to overall results by comprehensive schooling that had raised the age of selection from 11-plus. Also due to the initially unitary GCSEs at 16 plus which Joseph reluctantly introduced in 1986.

Although it replaced the former separation between O-level sheep and CSE goats at 14 plus, differentiated GCSE examinations were soon introduced bringing the age of selection down again. The Standard Assessment Tests at the four 'key stages' of the National Curriculum reintroduced testing and more testing lower down the schools. This contributed to, after 1988, the academic treadmill that teachers and their students found themselves on with the result that, especially as long as youth unemployment remained high and prospects uncertain, for many young people 'Education without jobs' replaced Finn's *Training Without Jobs*.

Conclusion: comprehensive education and the working class

It was certainly the case that 'the thirty glorious years' of full employment that followed the end of the Second World War allowed education to expand as part of the welfare state and encouraged limited progress towards lessening inequality. Opportunities were opened for more people to progress to further and higher levels. Even though the reforms were slow and remained incomplete, they were subject to consistent opposition. Struggling against this, many practitioners sought to engage working-class students to make comprehensive schools more than simply 'grammar schools for all.' Teachers continued to encourage mixed ability teaching and to broaden narrow academic approaches. As a result, overall attainment rose, especially in the most comprehensive regions such as Scotland and Wales, as opposed to those English boroughs and counties where selection of a minority persisted, depressing the aspirations of the majority.

However, if comprehensive education was a significant gain for the working class and should be seen as on a par with the creation of the National Health Service, the extent to which it changed working-class aspirations about work and society or, at least for the majority, seriously altered their place within it should not be overestimated. Being able to be educated in a comprehensive school with a range of different children, rather than under the custodial regime of the secondary modern or the often stultifying atmosphere of the grammar school, was clearly a significant factor in both raising aspirations and breaking down working-class hostility towards state education. Yet for much of the post-war period life went on as before for the majority of working-class students and education remained marginal as they left school for what employment they could find.

For example, even in the mid-1970s, forty per cent of students quit school with no recognised educational qualifications. For many working-class students the attractions of earning far outweighed those of learning and, as result, for many young people the raising of the school leaving age to 16 in 1972, was as much of an unnecessary distraction as one-and two-year YTS subsequently became. Or as a year or two intermittent attendance at sixth form or further education—normal though this now is—has become today. As this chapter has emphasised, it was the lack of employment opportunities for 16 year-old school leavers and the ending of the traditional English apprenticeship system with the collapse of heavy industry that determined the changes in the relationship between working-class school students and education.

As the following chapters will make clear, the education policies of successive Conservative and New Labour governments have been a response to the changing conditions faced by working-class youth. The period of MSC domination, in which billions of pounds were spent on 'training' a generation of young people to not only accept unemployment but also to see it, at least in part, as a reflection of their own inadequacies, was no exception. Comprehensive schools have survived but as the direction of education policy changed, many, particularly those in the inner city, have remained 'comprehensive' in name only. The chapter that follows examines how education, in addition to reorganising the lives of jobless school leavers, played a large part in the wider reorganisation of British society by the Conservatives in the 1980s. As well as describing events, it will relate these to the wider framework described in the opening chapter, particularly to changes in the economy and to the ongoing process of class recomposition outlined previously.

Chapter 3

Making it worse—Education and
the Conservative offensive

The Conservatives eventually succeeded in imposing a new order on education with their 1988 Education Reform Act supplemented by the 1992 Further and Higher Education Act. The ERA replaced the welfare state settlement of schooling by the 1944 Act which left it to teachers in schools to decide what and how to teach. This was now prescribed in detail by the new 10 academic subject National Curriculum occupying over seventy per cent of the timetable with tests at 7, 11, 14 and 16. The Further and Higher Education Act extended the new form of central funding from the polytechnics to further education. Together the two Acts are an example of what political scientist Andrew Gamble referred to as the 'strong state' existing alongside, but also overseeing, the smooth working of the 'free economy.' This chapter shows how recognising that a new market-state has replaced the post-war welfare state not only makes sense of what has happened, it also reveals the contradictions that the new state formation contains and explains its unstable and unsustainable nature, enabling us to assess how to move forward from it without necessarily returning to the welfare state as it was.

Towards a new world order and a new market-state

On coming to power in 1979, Tory education policy built on the backlash against comprehensives begun by the Black Papers, sustained by the right-wing press and endorsed by last Old Labour Premier, Callaghan. The Tories acted quickly to halt comprehensive expansion by encouraging LEAs to continue with selection where it existed. They also introduced the selected places scheme subsidising students from state schools to attend private schools on a means-tested basis. This was an early example of the new mixed economy with its state subsidised private sector discussed below.

However, reforming education was not the first priority of the new administration. They had come to power on the slogan 'Labour isn't working' but their monetarist economic policies soon trebled unemployment. Faced with spiralling youth unemployment and consequent rioting in the early 1980s, the government cut social security entitlements and reduced trainee allowances before making one and then two-year YTS compulsory. As we have already recounted, rather than disbanding the sprawling MSC bureaucracy as they had promised, the Tories replaced the Youth Opportunities Programme with a new £1 billion Youth Training Scheme.

But if education reform was placed on the back burner while they concentrated on 'training', the Tories were busy elsewhere. By the time the ERA and the National Curriculum were to reach the statute books, Mrs. Thatcher was well advanced in her project of rolling back the pillars of post-war social democracy and the welfare state. She had granted council tenants the 'right to buy', promoted the virtues of private health care and had set about privatising the public utilities. This followed the floatation of successive nationalised industries at knock-down prices for transnational corporations in newly deregulated global money markets awash with speculative capital. By ending progressive taxation, Thatcher not only rewarded these speculators but engineered a huge transfer of wealth from the poor to the rich within the UK. Social polarities were heightened, especially between regions like the North and South and between localities within all regions.

Most significantly, the Thatcher government beat the National Union of Mineworkers in a year-long civil war of attrition. Despite the decline in the strategic importance of coal, the miners were still the backbone of the trade union movement and in Thatcher's own words, 'the enemy within.' Their defeat altered the balance of power between social classes and cleared the decks for an American-style flexible labour market. It also destroyed the largest remaining productive heavy industry and the traditional way of life of the manual working class that went with it.

The defeat at home coincided with what proved to be the final disintegration abroad of the Soviet Union. There were mass movements against the cruel parody that socialism had become in Eastern Europe, along with defeat of the revolt against a similar future in China. The eventual victory of the U.S.A. in the Cold War revivified capitalism and seemed to leave no alternative to its rapacious plundering of the world and deepening impoverishment of its peoples. Under the remaining superpower, a single global market was reconstituted for the first time since 1914.

In the UK as elsewhere, private monopoly capital had become dominant over state capital. The compromise between them in the post-war welfare state settlement was overturned. This was the essence of the new market-state that was imposed by Mrs. Thatcher's governments. In place of clear divisions in the old 'mixed economy' between private and public sectors, a 'new mixed economy' indiscriminately mixed together a state-subsidised private sector that was now dominant over a semi-privatised state sector. Instead of consensus and compromise, a new centralised form of state administration now operates on the contracting principle borrowed from business. As responsibility for delivery is contracted out to institutions, power contracts to central government agencies which set targets enforced through inspection. Great Britain plc is run like a gigantic holding company.

Incessant inspection and surveillance of computerised accounting through endless paper trails become necessary in the 'audit culture' accompanying this change. They ensure that agents are actually meeting the targets set by the controlling agencies and not just pretending to meet them. Professional judgement of quality is reduced to mechanical costing of quantity. Turning everything into numbers that allows easy comparison is a form of commodification. It does not matter whether actual prices are attached to the more or less arbitrary quantitative measures of 'kwality', as Ted Wragg used to call it. The numbers already represent monetary value to the tax-paying 'consumer' of state services. New information and communications technology only helped to facilitate these facile comparisons, reducing things to numbers.

Meanwhile, the mines and factories inherited from the industrial revolution were asset stripped and replaced by the warehouses and shopping malls of the service sector as industrial and other labour has been 'outsourced.' With low wage part-time contract working replacing many of the 'proper' jobs of the past, especially for men, overall skill levels in employment actually declined, despite all the official emphasis on training. However, new technology offered new employment opportunities for women as well as for men in offices and sales. This was the shiny new plastic future for which education was to prepare its pupils and students.

Nationalising the school curriculum

Ironically, the Tories faced the new world order by reverting to a ten subject academic National Curriculum that re-imposed a grammar school curriculum on every school (substituting only 'technology' for 'Latin' in the 1902 regulations). Dangerous subjects such as sociology were pruned and even history would be lucky to survive (beyond 14 at least). A compulsory core curriculum seems to contradict 'free market' competition between educational 'providers', as schools, colleges and universities were becoming. Its Fordist model offers 'consumers', as parents and students were becoming, 'any colour car as long as it is black', rather than the post-Fordist notion of individual choice—or 'personalised provision' as it became.

In fact, Kenneth Baker, the Minister who was architect of the ERA, had to overcome the objections of fundamentalist free-marketeers within the factionalised Tory Party to his nationalisation of the curriculum. The argument has gone on since, resulting in a successive whittling down of the National Curriculum to a reduced core. At the same time, various different interests seek to load into it their compulsory references to anything from 'citizenship' (eventually accorded five per cent of secondary National Curriculum time) to the basic sex education that survived after Mrs. Thatcher banned reference to gay and lesbian relations for fear of 'promoting homosexuality.'

The traditional academicism of the National Curriculum was similar to the Conservatives' harking back to the lost world of the 1950s as they attempted to recreate a schools system mirroring the tripartite social divisions that used to exist between traditional upper, middle and working classes. New Labour were to prove much more adept at establishing a more subtle and flexible 'correspondence' between educational institutions and reconstituted social divisions. Still, the habitual division of provision into three types recurred in the various forms of tripartism New Labour was to sustain and elaborate at tertiary level, as well as at secondary and even primary level.

Before proceeding with their 'Great Education Reform Act', as Baker called it, the Tories had seen off national action by teacher trade unions in pursuit of improved pay. But not before the teachers had drawn blood in forcing the resignation of Baker's predecessor, Sir Keith Joseph. He was the brains behind Thatcher's visceral reactions—she was never the same without him. As a result of this defeat, new national conditions of service had been imposed on teachers. The Burnham Committee, where teachers' pay had been negotiated was replaced by an unaccountable and unrepresentative Pay Review Body.

Nevertheless, well over a year of action, including strikes, refusing to cover for absences and withdrawing from out of school activities, had developed a much harder trade union consciousness amongst teachers. School union groups collected money for striking miners and NUM officials addressed union conferences. But demobilising teachers and in particular marginalising the NUT, proved to be an important precondition for the success of the Conservative education project.

With its ethnocentric assumptions and the emphasis it gave to nationalist versions of British history and English literature (at the expense of more critical approaches in the social sciences), the National Curriculum was an overtly Conservative curriculum. It became the central plank of what Ken Jones, in his 1989 analysis of Conservative policy, called the *Right Turn* in educational politics. The National Curriculum assumed the unproblematic existence of a unified national culture that could be imposed on all sections of society. It thus ignored the possibility that students might bring a variety of (multi-)cultural and different class experiences to school. Its tightly prescriptive nature also enabled the small rightwing think tanks that Thatcher relied on for intellectual justification for her prejudices to have a disproportionate influence over what children learned in the classroom. (Not their own children of course since the National Curriculum did not apply to private schools!)

Ironically, the National Curriculum also took on a modernising role. In contrast to the haphazard way in which learning had been organised in the post-war years, it set out a curriculum 'entitlement.' It was this idea of a universal entitlement that sold it to teachers despite their reservations and even if this was only entitlement to 'a grammar schooling for all.' This was therefore yet another perversion of the comprehensive principle of equal opportunities for all.

The various 'key stage' benchmarks with their levels and performance indicators would, the proponents of the new curriculum argued, promote greater accountability. For the first time, parents received a booklet from the government about what would be learned in school, how it would be assessed and at what standard their children should be expected to perform. This had unanticipated consequences as, for example, the National Curriculum requirement that all students take maths, science and technology increased attainment by girls in these subjects as well as in the languages and arts that they already opted for.

Yet for large numbers of teachers and students, the experience of the National Curriculum was of a top heavy bureaucratic nightmare. The 'one size fits all' approach to learning reduced any incentive to be creative or innovative. It encouraged, if not necessitated, 'teaching to the test' with a culture of what Tom Davies calls 'taskism' in the classroom (see page 91). Almost from its inception, pressure grew for its reform. The most notable example was the 1993 SATs boycott by teacher unions. This resulted in the first of Sir Ron Dearing's reviews.

Dearing, a retired former-manager of the Post Office, recommended reducing the amount of prescription and streamlining the process of assessment. He also recommended vocational alternatives for those 15 and 16-year-old (now Key Stage 4) students identified as being 'disaffected.' This proposal signalled a retreat from the comprehensive promises of the National Curriculum with a return to the academic-vocational divisions of the previous MSC-dominated vocational training phase of education policy initiated by the Ruskin speech in 1976. The idea that there should be a different class of curriculum for different classes of students was favoured by traditional Conservatives. It would in the future also be key for New Labour. It marked a return to ancient atavisms of selection by supposed genetic inheritance.

Uniformity and diversity

While nationalising the curriculum, the ERA set up mechanisms for increasing diversity between schools. It did this by establishing an 'internal market' in education. This was an important concession to the free-market faction in the Conservative Party unhappy about the increased state direction of the curriculum. As seen, the ERA loosened the control of then-mainly Labour controlled Local Education Authorities over schools. It not only required LEAs to delegate most of the schools' budget to school governing bodies but it went further, encouraging schools to hold parental ballots to 'opt out' of the LEA. They could then become 'grant maintained' and receive their funding directly from a central government Funding Agency for Schools. The polytechnics and City Technology Colleges (see further) already did this, following the MSC model of funding for YTS. This 'incorporation' was extended to further education under its own Funding Council by the 1992 Act. Open enrolment for schools was also introduced to make it easier for governing bodies to increase the size of their intake and benefit from a funding regime based on a 'bums on seats' formula. Resourcing schools and colleges according to their size rather than social need has continued to provide the basis for funding under New Labour, who also applied the same funding method to universities.

Open enrolment drew on traditional right-wing Conservative arguments about 'parental choice.' As schools devoted more resources to marketing their services, parents, rather than working in partnership with schools, became consumers, or even 'customers.' The 1992 White Paper *Choice and Diversity* extended these initiatives and made it easier for schools to 'opt out' as only a small minority had so far done so. It also drew up Draconian procedures for dealing with 'failing schools' by strengthening the role of OfSTED, the national inspectorate established in 1990 and charged with enforcing the Tories' agenda in schools.

In the meantime, parents had been issued with a 'Charter'. Amongst other things, this promised regular publication of data about each schools' performance. As a result, 'league tables' began to appear in local and national newspapers. Later, Charters appeared for further education and higher education students along with (under New Labour) league tables of universities and subjects of study within them. The Tories also set national targets for the overall level of school performance, notably the ridiculous expectation that eighty per cent of students would gain five A-C GCSEs by 2000—a target that was revised downwards by New Labour to fifty per cent by 2002. Centrally imposed targets, with or without electoral mandates for them, became typical of the contracting administration of the new market-state with auditors and inspectors chasing the 'providers' to 'deliver' them.

Taking it further and higher

At first, marketisation and businessification was most visible in further education. Here, after the 'incorporation' of colleges in 1993, learning became a national 'business' rather than a local community service. Though the new college corporations had charitable status and were still dependent on public funding, they were allowed to enter into commercial contracts, to supply goods and services, acquire and dispose of land and property. They could also borrow from commercial markets and invest.

With these new powers, college principals quickly took on the functions of 'Chief Executives', as they nearly all now called themselves. Urged on by government, they adopted a business-style management culture of a most extreme form. Their colleges as businesses operated to maximise student numbers and guarantee funding as the 'price' of each 'funding unit' (i.e. student) was reduced. Costs were cut so that where possible lecturers' salaries reflected new local market rates rather than national agreements. The 1973 'Silver Book' agreement between staff unions and LEAs was thus abandoned after a long and bitter struggle.

The new form of administering the colleges through their own Further Education Funding Council for England(the FEFC) again illustrated the contracting principles of the new market-state. Alongside 'Next Step' agencies now controlling most civil services, a spaghetti soup of acronymic 'agencies', 'teams', 'trusts' and 'corporations' took over large parts of the local and national state, including the health service, urban development and parts of housing. They made up what Tony Blair as Opposition Leader called 'the Quango state' and which, like Mrs. Thatcher before she came into office, he pledged to abolish. These 'quasi-autonomous non-governmental bodies' (later called 'non-governmental agencies') now disburse over a quarter of all state funding. How much each of them receives is decided by the central government's Treasury whose power is further increased in this new state.

Like the Funding Council for Higher Education in England, together with the Funding Agency for (opted-out) Schools that the Conservatives also set up, the FEFC was a 'big quango.' The Chair of the 1994 Nolan Committee on standards in public life numbered these at 3,000 with 42,000 appointments to their boards (Radio Four 16 May 1996). The Secretary of State for Education appointed thirteen large private company representatives to the FEFC, like its first Chair who was a former-Chief Executive of Boots the Chemist. Putting such businesspersons in charge of public education was taken further when the FEFC was abolished by yet another 'training revolution.' It was taken over to form an even bigger quango, the employer-dominated Learning and Skills Council. Today this jockeys for power and influence with HEFCE in determining the future of further and higher education (see further).

College corporations are amongst the 'little quangos' that Lord Nolan also investigated. As independent individual agencies, they entered into contracts with the FEFC/LSC and other funding bodies to deliver services agreed in advance. Delivery is guaranteed by the achievement of various specified performance indicators. Responsibility for delivery is thus devolved downwards whilst power shifts upward. The new type of state, exemplified by the new governance of further education, is thus (as said) 'contracting' in two senses. As well as contracting with their funding councils, agencies like college corporations can in their turn contract out to other providers of services.

Through these administrative and accounting arrangements the rigours of the market were introduced—in further education as elsewhere—into previously local authority run and locally democratically controlled public services. The argument for this was that these services would be provided to their customers more cheaply, quickly, efficiently and responsively by a local—and national—semi-privatised state sector imbued not only with the ideology of enterprise but reorganised along the lines of the new, slimmed down, flexible, private sector in place of old and hierarchical state bureaucracies.

The same arguments were applied to higher education. As part of the 1992 Further and Higher Education Act, the Conservatives also inflicted significant changes on higher education. Rather than their initial approach of encouraging two-year degree courses and cutting higher education, pausing only to subsidise the private University of Buckingham (also with two-year degrees), the government set targets for higher education expansion. It was to cater for a third of all 18-21 year-olds by the year 2000.

Polytechnics and later some other higher education colleges, which had also been removed from LEA control, were granted 'university' status and allowed to award their own degrees. This doubled the number of university students at a stroke! Allowing the polytechnics to call themselves universities also disguised the fact that, as Tyrrell Burgess wittily said at the time, the universities were turning into polytechnics. As in further education, a new system of funding of labyrinthine incomprehensibility linked state funding by HEFCE to student numbers. This encouraged the new 'post 1992' universities and others to make up for the research funding enjoyed by some of their more established counterparts by recruiting as many students as possible. As in further education, they piled them high, especially on cheap and easy to deliver courses.

The freezing of student maintenance grants in the 1990s with the introduction of loans also prepared the way for the future introduction of tuition fees. The serviceable Lord Dearing suggested these in his third review, this time of higher education. His recommendations were accepted by a cross-Party consensus irrespective of the outcome of the 1997 general election. A new and more market-based admissions procedure with new divisions between what were to become referred to as the 'researching' and 'teaching', or 'selecting' and 'recruiting', universities, were anticipated by a group of traditional institutions. They secured their position at the top of the pecking order by forming 'the Russell Group'—a potential Ivy League some or all of whose members could eventually privatise themselves out of the state system. If/when this happens, the remaining majority of higher education institutions could be taken over and funded by a merged HEFCE and LSC, making further and higher education indistinguishable at this level. The original binary line within higher education would then have been redrawn much higher up the hierarchy. As it is, despite the opposition of a 'McDonald's Group' of former-polytechnics, in the worst of both worlds, mass universities for the many are already combined with élite universities for the few.

Unfortunately, such is the isolation and sectoral parochialism dividing schools from further education and higher education, that the negative lessons for lecturers of the incorporation of colleges were not learnt by their colleagues in schools and universities. The essential similarity of their situations was not apparent in competing 'providers of learning and skills' (as the further education colleges were now officially called). A single educational trades union across schools, colleges and universities, like the Educational Institute of Scotland, would have helped to bring about a more single vision. It is to be hoped that the recent merger of the former college and polytechnic teachers' union, NATFHE, with the Association of University Teachers to form the new University and College Union will contribute to such a unity of purpose. So too would moves towards a single school teachers' union. In the meantime, it is part of the purpose of this book to demonstrate the similarities of the situation of all those now teaching, researching and studying in the new system of education and training in England and to encourage discussion of how we can change it.

Education with 'McJobs'

For many, including some Tories, Conservative education policy appeared to be an uneasy compromise between centralisation and moves towards increased local diversity, or between the new right and free market factions within the increasingly divided Party. However, despite these tensions and contradictions that this chapter has explained in terms of a strong state presiding over a free market, Tory education policy was primarily a response to the broader social and economic changes outlined in the first chapter of the book. It was these changes, rather than the particular form which education policy has taken, that were the driving force behind both Conservative and New Labour initiatives of the last thirty years.

The 1990s saw more of the changes in the occupational structure that have already been referred to. In particular, the growth of white-collar employment, both in the administrative/managerial and technical/professional categories more likely to recruit on the basis of recognised exam qualifications. This and the erosion of the traditional manual/non-manual divide so marked in the post-war social and educational settlement by what chapter one described as an increasingly disjointed 'working-middle' of society, was a further reason for the increased significance of qualifications for labour market entry. The chapter referred to the way in which qualifications as 'skill assets' rather than local characteristics, family contacts, or what were referred to as 'organisational assets', were becoming more important in recruitment to a significant number of jobs.

But as the first chapter also made clear, it should not be assumed that the qualifications sought by employers necessarily encompass the particular skills or social attributes that correspond with changes in the economy—in other words a new human capital. On the contrary, education credentials can simply serve as screening devices, providing information to employers about an applicant's educational track record. They provide a means of helping employers decide which candidates they should interview and which they should not.

Qualifications became proxies for skills, despite the efforts in the 1980s by a sub-agency of the MSC to create new National Vocational Qualifications. NVQs were based upon the behavioural competences actually required to perform various tasks in employment. The impossible 'vision' of the MSC of 'bridging the skills gap' was to provide an exact correspondence between training 'outcomes' from schools and colleges and those competences required by employers for specific tasks. The delusion lives on in today's Sector Skills Council and the 'skills agenda' of the New Labour government. They claim that their new vocational qualifications, alongside traditionally academic qualifications, can meet the challenges of employment in what the Tories originally referred to as 'a learning society.'

The socio-economic changes encapsulated by this particularly silly slogan reflected the fact that the eighteen years of Conservative government coincided with significant increases in staying on rates and also rapid improvements in examination performance. By 1992 for example, only thirteen per cent of 16-17 year-olds had full-time jobs and DfES figures showed that the proportion of those staying in full-time education after 16 rose from 51.5 per cent to 69.3 per cent in the ten years after the passing of ERA. During the Conservative years the number of 17-year-olds remaining in education increased from under 25 per cent to over 60 per cent. Whereas in the mid-1970s, as stated, over forty per cent of students left school without any educational qualifications, by the end of the 1990s the same number were leaving with 5 GCSE A-C grades.

Thus, if education had become an increasingly important arena for government intervention, rising participation and performance also confirmed that young people had began to re-evaluate the importance of education as a means for labour market progression and social survival if not social mobility. Rather than representing an endorsement or confirming the success of Conservative education policies, it is more accurate to say that this revaluation took place in spite of them. Nor do the changed attitudes shared by many young people meet the ideals of a 'learning society' held for them by enthusiasts for more education reform and more 'modernisation.'

For example, changes in labour market opportunities have also profoundly influenced the way more and more students now view higher education. For previous generations of predominantly traditionally middle-class students, going to university was a valued activity in itself, regardless of the employment opportunities it assuredly opened up. It was also financed at the tax payer's expense (although progressive taxation meant that if graduates earned more, they also paid more tax—like anybody else).

By contrast, for a group of inner London GNVQ students interviewed at the end of the 1990s, 'uni' was seen as essential for 'getting a better position', having 'better respect' and avoiding a life of 'Sainsbury's jobs'—the work they already did on a part-time basis but which they hoped success in education would lead them away from. Qualifications were needed not because these students expected to achieve extensive social mobility but simply because it was what you now had to do.

One thing shared by all students and trainees at all levels of study, save the minority who might once have progressed via academic sixth form to traditional higher education, was that thirty years ago most of them would not have been in any sort of post-compulsory education at all. This is obvious to many students, including the 16-year-old resitting her GCSEs at an inner city further education college in 1992 who said:

> 'you have to work harder and harder to get a worse and worse job. You have to go to university to get what thirty years ago you didn't even have to have A-levels for.'

Many similar students would nowadays proceed to a local university. There they take courses in the subject areas of their GNVQs, often business studies or ICT. Continuing to live at home and carrying on with their part-time employment that they began during sixth form or before, these youngsters constitute a new kind of university student in a new working-middle class.

In being a response to the collapse of the post-war 'consensus' and to the failure of youth training schemes to provide anything more that *Training Without Jobs*, the Education Reform Act represented an attempt to impose a new 'settlement' on young people. This time, instead of warehousing young people on Youth

Training Schemes, they are warehoused in 'education without jobs.' Or rather, in the new post-Fordist and post-industrial economy, in education combined with 'McJobs' as well. Often, given the oversupply of certified if not qualified labour, they are in danger of graduating to 'McJobs'. Copying the German 'dual system' of providing either education or workplace vocational training, as in the MSC phase of things, has been dropped. In its place, a U.S. model has been adopted with the aim of keeping as many young people in full-time education as possible. And if they can be made to pay for the privilege, so much the better for the emerging *Business of Learning*.

Under New Labour the pursuit of academic qualifications has intensified and in some ways the issue of educational success has been given a new dimension. For example, the government has continued to emphasise the importance of education in terms of promoting individual social mobility, but also, in the absence of any more general redistributive policies, as a new way of securing social justice. Elsewhere, New Labour have continued with or even extended the internal market and encouraged the privatisation of educational provision. Above all, they have continued to depend on a highly directive centralised state. The chapter that follows evaluates New Labour policies and demonstrates the need for alternatives to them.

Chapter 4

Putting it right or making it even worse? New Labour's new ideas

It did not matter which of the two main Parliamentary Parties won the 1997 election. On the night the results were announced, the Adam Smith Institute held a 'Victory for the Free Market' celebration without radio or TV to report the results. Similarly, the last edition before the election of the U.S. magazine *Newsweek* (28 April 1997) featured a cover picture of Baroness Thatcher with the title 'The Real Winner.' As neo-Thatcherites, New Labour government consolidated the new market-state more effectively than Major's government could manage. Nevertheless, the government was overtaken by the same contradictions as dogged John Major. In particular, the new mixed economy of state-subsidised private monopoly capital dominant over semi-privatised state capital made the same sleezy corruption endemic. More generally, as public services like education were perverted into market providers, their ethos was changed towards commercial values. This was part of a general commodification of society that New Labour aimed to take much further than even Mrs. Thatcher had dared to do.

From full employment to 'full employability'

Well before their 1997 election victory, the New Labour Party had insisted that 'education, education, education' would be at the heart of their new government. They argued this was the best economic policy in the new post-industrial/post-Fordist global marketplace where education now had an unprecedented role in securing national economic prosperity through investment in human capital. Human capital was supposedly even more important than the classical conception of capital as money, land, or plant and machinery because inspirational new ideas were now the secret to success. They could help UK plc adapt flexibly in new niche markets in the fast changing global economy. Especially as old-style factory production had been exported abroad to low wage countries like China and India, along with the hard labour of the industrial past.

Central to New Labour's thinking about changes in the economy was an acceptance that the state could no longer intervene against market forces to guarantee 'full employment' in the way that Old Labour and 'One Nation' Tories used to do. Keynesian demand management of the national economy was out as the state could now only respond to the supply side to 'shape advantage' and prepare people for 'full employability'. In an internationally competitive labour market well paid jobs would be available for those who had invested sufficiently in their own human capital through high levels of education and training.

As an 'enabling state' the government could only, in the words of a 1997 White Paper, offer *Excellence for Everyone*. The more people who took advantage of these opportunities that the state afforded them, the wealthier the economy would be as it attracted international finance capital to fund these new niche products and the high level skills and knowledge they would need. This was 'the third way' New Labour promised between the old bureaucratic state planning of the past and the 'on your bike' attitude of the uncaring Conservatives' free-market competition.

Old Labour too had stressed the importance of education in the production of human capital. Indeed, we have seen that this was a prime justification for Old Labour's comprehensive schools policy and for expanding technical and higher education. This also had a social justification in overcoming class and other differences to offer equal opportunities for all. But for New Labour the relationship was much more pronounced and more specific.

Government policy documents emphasised the way in which the 'Fordist' economy based on mass production and the repetition of relatively straight forward tasks had supposedly given way to post-Fordism based on 'flexible production'. This required workers to be multi-skilled and able to respond to an economy where consumer demands were continually changing. Policy statements also emphasised how the old assumptions about having 'a job for life' had been superseded by expectations that people would move not only from job to job on a regular basis but also from sector to sector. As a result, not only would higher levels of education be essential, but 'lifelong learning' was also necessary as everyone would have to continually 're-skill' themselves simply to keep up. That the state offered help to enable people to do this was the social dimension of New Labour's third way.

If individuals did not take advantage of these opportunities to be unequal, they had only themselves to blame for their continuing 'social exclusion'. Thus there was to be 'no fifth option' of remaining unemployed on restored benefits under New Labour's much trumpeted New Deal that it immediately offered unemployed youth and others. This financed its four options with a windfall tax on the superprofits of the privatised public utilities sold off to 'Fat Cats' by the Conservatives.

However, as the first chapter argued, New Labour's assertions were largely ideological. Debate continues about how effective the New Deal actually was since the economy was picking up anyway at the time of its launch. Certainly, globalisation provided relatively few openings for those with high levels of education and skills, as opposed to employers demanding inflated levels of certification for more and more jobs. On the contrary, it was the lack of opportunities for young people leaving school to find worthwhile employment which was the primary reason for greater participation in education. The previous chapter also noted that the increases in staying-on rates had taken place despite Conservative education policies that sought to undermine both comprehensive ideals and equal opportunities.

New Labour and the 'standards' agenda

The 1997 White Paper *Excellence in Schools* detailed New Labour's aggressive campaign to raise performance levels and 'standards.' More performance data would be published, from baseline assessment of five year-olds to local league tables for SATs and GCSEs. Primary and secondary schools, under the auspices of their LEA would be required to set challenging targets, while OfSTED, under its hated head, the ultra-conservative Chris Woodhead, was given increased powers to tackle 'failing schools.'

Woodhead's retention was a clear signal of intent to teachers, an indicator of continuity as clear as Blair sending his own children to an opted-out secondary school. Most school teachers lost any illusions that they had entertained of the new government at this early stage. Ever since, state schooling has been run like a huge corporation—an 'Education plc', where thousands of outlets (schools), inspected and policed by OfSTED, report to local managers (LEAs), who are in turn regulated by a powerful headquarters (the DfES).

Excellence in Schools also emphasised the intention of 'modernising' comprehensive schools. It denounced 'mixed ability' teaching as a failure and promoted setting, 'fast tracking' and the advantages of accelerated learning to differentiate 'gifted and talented pupils' from the rest. Comprehensive schools with their 'one size fits all' approach of equal opportunities were declared hopelessly old fashioned ('modernist' instead of 'postmodernist'/'Fordist' instead of 'post-Fordist'). As the Green Paper *Schools: Building on Success* (DfEE 2001, 15) stated:

'In the twenty-first century we need to change this to build a flexible system around the needs and aspirations of individual pupils and their families ...'

But still New Labour was unable to actually repudiate the comprehensive principle and argue for a return to openly selective schooling because everyone knew this implied secondary modern schooling for the majority who failed. The electorate had after all just rejected John Major's proposal for 'a grammar school in every town.' Instead, the comprehensive principle was perverted through its modernisation. Similarly, although econometric testing differentiated pupils, according to their various 'aptitudes' if not abilities, into different 'learning styles' and in a hundred even less subtle ways, the crude IQ test of supposedly inherited 'general intelligence' was not yet generally invoked.

Schools as well as pupils were also to improve and reach ever higher academic standards. New Labour had identified themselves closely with the school effectiveness and school improvement movement. This had become current in academic educational research thanks in large part to the London University Institute of Education which announced its own importance by denouncing 'producer capture' of schools by teachers. Educational researchers claimed to be able to identify the factors that create 'effective schools'—particular types of management structure, leadership and communication styles, which can, it was argued, be used everywhere to the same effect.

In other words, the problem of low attainment by sections of the school population is considered to be primarily a technical or managerial question. It is not a consequence of wider social inequalities. This approach is class, gender, disability and colour blind. Appeal to such well established social differences is considered a mere 'excuse for underperformance.' The national performance levels of all pupils could therefore be driven up if schools 'improve.' Negative sanctions—ultimately closure—for those that fail to do so would ensure that they did. LEAs, colleges and later universities could all be subject to the same approach with the same reliance on standardised data returns.

It would be wrong to deny that certain types of management structures can 'make a difference' to how effective schools are but theories of school improvement fit neatly with the more general model of measuring educational performance outlined above. According to critics of school improvement, the difference between more effective and less effectively managed schools seems to account for between eight to fifteen per cent of the differences in student performance. But even this would not be enough to explain the emphasis given to targeting those students just outside the all important five GCSE A-C grades. Once again, performance changed to meet the targets that were set. More inspection and audit is then required to ensure that teachers and lecturers are not fiddling the figures. Professional judgement is overruled and the only autonomy allowed is whatever is necessary to meet the standards that have been set.

New Labour and teachers

However, compared with the Conservatives largely punitive approach, New Labour's policies for teachers have been more strategic. By using 'performance management' indices, Labour has been able to link teachers' pay and career progression to the progress of their students and to performance targets set for their schools. These measures have been designed to change the culture of teaching and to facilitate the move from a collective professionalism to an atomised and fragmented schools workforce. For example, the General Teaching Council that New Labour established in 1999, is far from being the self-governing professional body that teacher unions had long campaigned for. It is instead a partially representative hybrid organisation with which teachers are compelled to register while at the same time it regulates their conduct and serves as a transmission belt for successive government policy initiatives. More like a company union than anything else.

Similar 'professional bodies' were set up for further education and higher education whose lecturers were lumped together under the same Sector Skills Council as youth and community, careers and adult education workers. Far from having responsibility for their own registration and training, like other professional organisations, school teachers already had their own Teacher Training (later Training and Development) Agency to dictate the competences they were supposed to meet on post-graduate certificate of education programmes delivered in schools, colleges and higher education. (Later, doctors were to receive the same treatment, not just through the new contract for GPs but with the 2006 Department of Health *Good Doctors, Safer Patients* proposals to abolish the role of the General Medical Council to set the content of the undergraduate medical curriculum in favour of yet another government agency.)

New Labour have also set about 'remodelling the teaching workforce', transferring an increasing number of tasks, including cover for absences, to teaching assistants. This allowed more time for teachers to concentrate on 'raising standards' in the classroom but in the process created a two tier teaching force. In further education, there was similar reliance on growing numbers of lower-paid agency supplied teachers, while in higher education many undergraduate courses are taught by post-graduate part-timers alongside contract researchers on fixed-term contracts.

Under the *Every Child Matters* agenda that brings together local authority education with social services in a unified administration which could then be outsourced, staff could be transferred from one sector, such as health, to another, such as education. What Nick Grant (2005, 23) calls the 'naïve ignorance about and a lack of strategy to overcome the historically entrenched beliefs and practices of the differing children's workforces' results in the practical difficulties involved in such partnership working. These were illustrated by the Connexions strategy, bringing together in a 'one stop shop' all those involved in providing services for young people. 'Rolled out' nationwide in 1999 and then rolled in again five years later at a cost which has still not been counted, the demise of 'Cx' leaves the future of youth services more than ever in doubt.

Connexions illustrates another feature of New Labour's 'experimental' and 'dynamic' approach, aside from funny spelling and dodgy acronyms. This is that provision in one area need not be the same as that in another, nor need it stay the same. As well as a speedy response, this approach is justified as encouraging flexibility to deliver new services and recombine old ones to meet changing social demand. The fluidity of the new arrangements encourages competition to meet these demands between the various 'partners' involved. But it does away with any consistent standards that could be statutorily expected to be provided, by schools for example. A similar erosion of entitlement has happened with devolution to hospital trusts in the NHS, which as a consequence can no longer accurately be described as a 'National' Health Service.

Meanwhile headteachers, like college principals and university Vice Chancellors, have become increasingly estranged from what goes on in their institutions due to changes in organisation and financial delegation. They operate their schools, colleges and universities as 'social enterprises' in partnership and competition with private and other public services in response to particular individual and group needs in innovative and flexible ways. They link with other agencies, expanding or disbanding the services they provide as circumstances change and as funding opportunities arise. Universities behave similarly in relation to research competition as well as to provide training services to local businesses, like colleges of further education.

This jostling for position by 'social entrepreneurs' could more accurately be described as 'hustling', as former-U.S. Labor Secretary, Robert Reich approvingly described the characteristic activity of 'the new economy' on BBC Radio 4's *Start the Week* (14 May 2001). It is typical of policy delivered by competing agencies bidding for contracts in the new market-state. The endemic insecurity and short-termism of the contract culture in which funds do not necessarily go to the most deserving but to those who write the best bids has been widely deplored (not only for research funding in higher education). The setting and auditing of performance indicators for specifically targeted initiatives has repeatedly been seen as systematically distorting. It inevitably results in 'All Pigs Flying' returns that are just too good to be true!

With some headteachers now being appointed to run a 'federation' of schools rather than just one, it has been suggested by one of the headteacher professional associations that for aspiring headteachers having a teaching qualification is less important than business or managerial expertise. Appointed, like some City businessmen, on short-term contracts to meet specific goals in exchange for incentive payments and supported by bursars to manage their accounts, each school recreates its own corporate bureaucracy accountable to its board of governors. They replace the democratically responsible LEA from whose centralised and more cost-effective 'red tape' schools have been 'freed.' As we have pointed out, the same happened previously in further education colleges.

Creating even more diversity: From Specialist Schools to Academies

New Labour came into office emphasising 'standards not structures.' This mantra was another clear indication that there would be no overall structural reform and that the Conservatives 'choice and diversity' agenda for different types of school would be maintained. New Labour therefore fudged bringing the Tory-sponsored Grant Maintained schools back under LEAs by creating a new category of Foundation Schools. These retained many of the powers gained by opting out. Then early in 2001, Blair's high profile press officer, Alastair Campbell, attacked 'bog standard' comprehensive schools and a pre-election Green Paper announced plans to dramatically expand the specialist schools programme.

All schools would now be encouraged to become 'specialist', on condition that they could raise an initial £50,000 from business sponsors. 'Faith Schools' for Anglicans, Catholics, Jews, Moslems, Hindus and other creeds were also encouraged. Parents too were supposed to be able to set up their own 'Charter Schools' on a model that had produced very mixed results in the U.S.A. New

Labour also set about expanding the City Academies programme. The post-election White Paper, *Schools Achieving Success*, proposed 20 such academies, reminiscent of the 20 self-governing and independently funded City Technology Colleges once promised by Kenneth Baker (see Beckett 2007). By 2005 there was a commitment to a further 200.

City Academies were to be 'independent' state schools like the CTCs. Not that the CTCs had materialised as Baker imagined in inner-city areas. They had though provided a model borrowed from Youth Training agencies for running all schools as independent trusts. Similarly, in exchange for an initial £2 million down-payment (all other costs being met by the state) sponsors were to be given control of the Academy and encouraged to develop their own particular 'ethos.' This included the teaching of 'creationism' by evangelical Christians.

The Academies programme has been the most controversial of all New Labour initiatives and the one to which there has been the most opposition. Academies are an example of New Labour's determination to induce 'diversity.' They are also a catalyst for privatisation and to replace LEAs as the main providers of education. Already Local *Education* Authorities no longer exist but as mere LAs they are now part of School Services or Children and Families Services with a Children's Trust beside or over them.

New Labour's critics have been correct to highlight the significance of private sector involvement in the Academies programme. Just as important has been the contribution of religious foundations and other non-profit making 'trusts.' Ealing NUT Secretary and anti-academies campaigner, Nick Grant, has made a useful distinction between those Academies set up to replace 'failing' working-class, inner city schools—where they have taken over from New Labour's previous Education Action Zones (EAZs)—and 'green field' Academies. These will be completely new schools in suburban or semi-rural locations.

> 'They will embody a new apartheid, two-tier system, as the equivalent of the grammar schools previous generations fought so hard to dismantle, even though it will be the level of resourcing and not selection by ability that will make them exceptional.'   (Grant, p. 40)

The 2006 Education Bill next created a new category of Trust schools. A half way house between Foundation Schools (ex-Grant Maintained) and the Academies, 'trusts' will also have external sponsors and be outside the LA. Like Academies, sponsors can include private companies. Churches and charities, private schools and universities have also shown an interest. Government is also encouraging federations of schools to become trusts. Like academies, trusts will largely control their own admissions policies, be able to set their own curriculum and appoint their own governing bodies. They are state-subsidised private schools.

The proposals to create Trust Schools became the main focus of opposition to the 2006 Education and Inspection Act. When originally proposed, it was implied that all new secondary schools, if not indeed all schools altogether, would have to become Trusts. However, as a result of a campaign that consisted primarily of Parliamentary lobbying and which led to up to sixty Labour MPs opposing the Bill so that it required Conservative opposition support to scrape through the Commons, the Trust proposals were watered down, though not scrapped. Now what will happen will probably vary from authority to authority but once the proportion of schools opting out for Trust status, doubtless encouraged by government incentives or bribes, reaches a critical threshold then the pressure on the remaining schools to follow suit will become irresistible.

Local admissions codes have also been tightened and Local Authorities allowed to submit bids for new schools. Unelected local Admissions Forums made up of local headteachers and school governors will decide on disputed cases when parents do not get the school of their choice. Similarly, centrally appointed Schools Adjudicators will judge the competition to provide a new school once this decision has been endorsed by the Secretary of State. New schools are only allowed under the Act if they increase 'diversity' and 'parental choice.' The 'parent power' promised by the legislation is slightly compromised by Trust schools having only one elected parent governor compared to as many as seven previously. This is supposedly compensated for by new Parent Councils in some Trust schools but these have only a consultative role.

Privatisation, privatisation, privatisation

Altering the role of the L(E)A changes it from a provider of education to a 'commissioner', or local brokerage system through which an array of providers can be put in touch with 'customers.' So increasing diversity has gone hand in hand with New Labour's enthusiasm for giving the private sector a commanding role. As under the Conservatives, the rationale given by government is the private sector's supposed contribution to innovation and efficiency. This justifies the significant part that business has played as a 'sponsor' or a 'partner' to these various initiatives.

However, alongside what Anderson and Hatcher refer to as a 'not for a profit activity', the provision of core services, in some cases the privatisation of the entire LA, has created an extensive and lucrative market. In Islington for example, Cambridge Education Associates (CEA) are now responsible for running the whole of the LA. Elsewhere, Nord Anglia and the U.S. company Edison have made huge inroads and correspondingly large profits as private sector providers.

As then-NUT National Executive member Bernard Regan argued, because it is unable to convince its own supporters that Local Authorities should be abolished, the Blair Government has set about dismantling them. When public disillusion results in Tory gains in local elections, the New Labour government is better able to deal with these more enthusiastic privatisers to outsource still further than with old Labour councils who typically drag their feet.

Building Schools for the Future (BSF) is another programme involving the private sector that will lead to a major expansion of the Private Finance Initiative. PFI is a financial arrangement where public service infrastructure is owned if not provided by contractors and then leased back to those who were once responsible for it. Introduced by the Tories in 1992, PFI has been revamped and forcefully promoted by New Labour as Public Private Partnership. The accountancy fraud involved in the way the Treasury under Gordon Brown has used PFI/PPP to discount public debt while tying tax payers to long-term repayments to private corporations has been widely exposed. So too have the shoddy buildings, equipment and services provided by some companies while others have gone broke leaving half-built schools and hospitals that still have to be paid for from the public purse. The National Health Service is particularly affected (see Pollock, 2004). From our point of view, all this represents a further instance of the take-over of public assets by private corporations and the dominance of private over state monopoly capital in the new market-state.

However, as Dexter Whitfield (2006) argues, markets in public services are rarely created in a single 'Big Bang.' Instead, they are stimulated by numerous policies and initiatives in parallel with the erosion of public services. As a result, marketisation and subsequent privatisation develops in different ways at different speeds in different services but in all cases the state plays a key role in creating and sustaining markets and in subsidising privatisation. Mrs. Thatcher took a 'Big Bang' approach to the privatisation of the nationalized industries but, with the exception of John Major's disastrous privatiation of British Rail in 1996, the pace of change has quickened since 1997 with New Labour's privatisation of the public services. To achieve this, New Labour operates simultaneously on many fronts, each of which feeds from and strengthens the others.

PFI/PPP for instance, having become embedded in the public sector, has spawned a secondary market for speculating in the public money involved, selling it on to other companies while developing derivative specialisms in the NHS Local Improvement Finance Trust and in BSF. But, according to Dexter, 'PFI has never been simply an alternative method of financing infrastructure investment'; it is part of 'a longer term strategy by which the private sector will ultimately own/control the welfare state and provide privatized core services.'

Thus BSF is not just about the provision of new schools. It illustrates Dexter's 'five-stage marketisation process': 1. commodifying services, 2. commodifying labour, 3. restructuring the state to 4. weaken democratic accountability and 5. embed business interests. Apart from extending opportunities to be part of PFI/PPP consortia for the first time to the educational and other business consultants reported in *The Guardian* (2 September 2006) as milking a record £2.2 billion from government contracts annually, BSF also drives LAs (or the Trusts of which they are a part) into a commissioning role in line with the government's longer-term strategy.

In his latest book, Dexter draws a diagram to show how teachers have been 'corralled' by academies, school trusts, BSF, the outsourcing of services like school meals, the childcare market, private supply agencies, commercialisation of materials with sponsorship of events and the privately controlled Local Educational Partnerships. As a result he says, 'Secondary and primary education may remain largely state funded for the foreseeable future, but they will be delivered mainly by private contractors.'

In Dexter's previous 2001 book, a chapter titled 'The nation state in 2020' shows where all this could eventually end with transnational corporations providing 'cradle to grave' health, education, social care and local environmental services with 'two-tier provision for all basic services.' With 'a myriad of tax reliefs, allowances, subsidies, vouchers and grants,' 'choice is determined by ability to pay.' 'Local government is reduced to a skeleton regulatory and monitoring agency' and 'Cities are run by elected mayors and committees of business people.' They assign staff to groups of contracts, not to particular sectors like health or education. Meanwhile, national government is 'limited to coordinating sponsorship and patronage by business and organising competitions and lotteries.' 'The [new market-] state is fluid, shapeless, functioning as provider, partner, client, contractor, financier and facilitator.'

Something like this was proposed in the U.S.A. as shown by an article in *The Economist* as long ago as 25 January 1997, which described 'A revolution in the administration of American poverty programmes ...' reporting that 'Anderson Consulting, the world's biggest consultancy, is bidding against Lockheed Martin, the world's largest defence contractor, for a five-year contract to run the entire Texas state welfare system.' As a result, 'Almost every aspect of welfare, from determining whether a claimant is eligible for help to preventing fraud and making payments, will eventually be in private hands', including job-training, drug-rehabilitation and pregnancy-prevention programmes, thirty social programmes in all, 'whose administration currently costs the state $550m a year.' Even though this proposal was subsequently defeated in Texas, the article added that 'Oregon, Maryland, and Wisconsin are already working along similar lines.' It should not be thought that such privatisations occur only under doctrinaire, Republican administrations. The welfare-reform law, signed by President Clinton, 'ending welfare as we know it' in his own words, in August 1996 allows states far more flexibility in their use of private contractors.

More recently *The Financial Times* (18 August 2006) reported 'Japan's public sector faces privatisation':

> 'Virtually every government service in Japan could be put out to tender in the biggest shake-up of the public sector in the country's history ... A law that came into force last month will allow public services to be 'market tested' to see if they could be better run in private hands ... Under the 'market testing' concept, direct comparisons will be made to see whether a service can be provided more efficient by the public or private sector. If a private company wins a tender, it will have three to five years to show it has run the service efficiently and met quality standards as a condition of being rewarded the contract ... Foreign companies can apply to run services, though none have done so yet.

Japan already incorporated all its public universities in 2004.

A Gradgrind curriculum for target-driven teaching

In line with their presentation of privatisation as 'modernisation', New Labour claim to want to 'modernise' the National Curriculum. However, apart from bringing in 'citizenship' as a distinctive subject, the government has concentrated its energies on introducing a series of 'strategies.' These have set out criteria for how the curriculum should be delivered but in some cases they have also stipulated how lessons should be taught including the pace at which they should be conducted. The Key Stage 3 strategy for example, splits lessons into 20-minute segments, all lessons commencing with 'starter activities' and ending with 'a plenary.'

The 'literacy strategy' starting in state primary schools has been particularly controversial. It includes a daily 'literacy hour' during which teachers are instructed to carry out specific activities for specific periods of time, for example, spending 15 minutes on sentence construction. The literacy strategy lays out what should be taught in each term and in this respect is even more prescriptive than the original National Curriculum. As Terry Wrigley observes (2006, 76), the literacy strategy is based on 'reading to order' and reinforced by cascade-type training, monitoring and a continuous stream of training videos, manuals, workbooks and websites to control teachers' decisions. Even when teachers are encouraged to use exploratory discussions, this is undermined by the number of objectives they have to cover. The emphasis on transmitting discrete skills and items of knowledge leads to didactic teaching where children's responses are tightly constrained.

On the basis of evidence from a relatively small-scale research project in Clackmannshire, Scotland—the results of which have been questioned by a number of other researchers—the importance of using 'synthetic phonics' as the one best way to teach reading, rather than as one of a number of teaching strategies, has also been mandated. All this, and especially the dreaded SATs for which preparations start terms in advance, have driven the joy out of primary teaching for both teachers and taught.

Nevertheless, the government would claim that its strategies have produced results: between 1995 and 2000 the percentage of 11-year-olds pupils awarded Level 4 or above rose from 48 per cent to 75 per cent in English and from 44 per cent to 72 per cent in maths. It is questionable whether performance has increased to the extent claimed. According to many critics, 'standards' have increased largely because of teachers 'teaching to the test.' The *Times Educational Supplement* (07 July 2006) for example, revealed that contributors to its online forum continually complained that key stage 2 English test results were way above their own assessments of their pupils. Rigorous comparison over time show that standards of spelling and maths are slipping (Shayer, forthcoming), while other contributors to the *TES* forum made accusations about a 'political agenda' to make results look good. More pigs flying!

In secondary schools, the estrangement of increasing numbers of students is vividly illustrated by Nick Grant's account of how a lesson about the historical reasons for why black people lived in the U.S.A. failed to get much of a response from his non-white Year-10 class because they had already 'done' slavery in Year-9. Grant recalls:

> 'These students sorted, filed and memorised their learning according to what was necessary to jump the hoops of a particular juncture of their lives.'   (p. 18)

His account could be replicated a thousand times in further education and higher education. As a student wrote in a final-year Education Studies degree project at Greenwich University in 2004, this is because 'Overassessment has made subject knowledge and understanding a thing of the past as students are put through a routine year after year, practising what exactly to write and where in preparation for exams.'

Grant's fellow Ealing NUT activist Tom Davies (in Grant 2005, 19) refers to this as 'taskism', where learning is reduced to the completion of predetermined and measurable tasks, satisfying undemanding criteria or requiring little engagement with students' surroundings. It can be compared to what Alan Ryan (2006, 96) calls 'teaching to the module' in higher education, resulting in what he calls

> 'a process of 'dumbing into the middle' by, in essence making teachers produce predictable, manageable, easily mastered modules, examined in predictable and easily mastered ways.'

Even very young children, now referred to as 'Early Years', have not been exempt from factory style schooling. 'Play', always at the centre of post-war 'Plowden' education, has been squeezed out at Key Stage 1 because of the continued pressure on the curriculum for less collaborative and more formal methods of teaching. A motion passed unanimously at the 2006 NUT Conference noted that 'the reduction in the opportunities for more informal play for children ... is having a detrimental effect on their social skills.' It contrasted government expenditure on electronic whiteboards with lack of initiatives 'for imaginative role play such as purchase of home corner equipment sand and water trays and playground climbing equipment' (www.teachers.org.uk). The government's direction was clear however in Gordon Brown's announcement in his first Budget speech that even 'childcare is now an integral part of economic development'! (although he was referring here primarily to crèches for parents).

A sign of things to come? New Labour's 'new' vocationalism

It is the top end of the secondary age group on which Labour promised to focus its attention for its third term. The 2006 Education and Inspections Act provided young people with an 'entitlement' to follow one of 14 specialist vocational diplomas from Year 10. They are the government's substitute for its failure to follow the Tomlinson Report recommendations which we mentioned in chapter one. Tomlinson offered a partial move towards unifying academic and vocational qualifications along the lines of Scottish highers that qualify 17-year-olds for entry to four years of university there and ensure many more stay on in further education or higher education. However, according to Qualifications and Curriculum Authority publicity, the new proposals, outlined in the 2005 *14-19* White Paper, are the most dramatic changes being made to the secondary curriculum anywhere in the world!

The government wants up to forty per cent of KS4 students to take one of the fourteen vocational diplomas. Pilots in five vocational areas will start from 2008, with all diplomas due to be up and running by 2013. Students will be able to take them at level 1 or 2. Level 2 will be equivalent to GCSE grade C and is designed to occupy about half of the total timetable. Level 1 can also be used in conjunction with the White Paper proposals for a new work-based learning route for 'disaffected' 14 plus students. At post-16, a level 1 and 2 diploma can be completed in a year and students will also be able to follow a two-year level 3 qualification which, like the current vocational qualifications, will occupy the majority of their study time. The government says that the diplomas will improve the quality and the reputation of vocational education with employers, universities and the public. They also want them to promote better workplace skills and have given the employer based Sector Skills Councils a lead role in diploma design.

Realising schools can only offer one or two of the fourteen different diplomas, government plan to create two hundred specialist vocational schools and in some cities, networks of Academies, part sponsored by local employers. Again, reminiscent of 1944 Act, this time of the technical or secondary modern schools rather than the grammars, they will be linked to local BSF initiatives. Here again the potential for direct private sector involvement is increased and compels LAs to accept them since this will be the only source of available funding.

But according to the 2005 Further Education White Paper, the number of KS4 students attending college for part of the week will also increase dramatically. As a result of the Increased Flexibility Programme up to 120,000 14-16 year-olds currently attend further education colleges for at least a day a week. With the DfES predicting that 350,000 14-16 year-olds will be enrolled on specialist diplomas, this number could double. Aside from complaints about children running amok in mainly adult colleges, further education lecturers who receive less pay than schoolteachers are less than enthusiastic about having to look after pupils they think the teachers no longer want to teach.

Rather than teaching any real understanding and despite a number of critical reviews, many vocational courses continue to be based on a very limited 'competence-based' conception of learning. This behavioural approach denies the need for any underpinning knowledge or for integrating competences into holistic skills. As noted, General National Vocational Qualifications were originally introduced as a compromise with the original narrow vision of competence embodied in occupationally specific NVQs (see chapters 1 and 3). Ironically, at the same time, higher level vocational qualifications, like advanced GNVQs, have drifted academically to function as entry qualifications for former-polytechnics. They have become 'applied' equivalents to the very qualifications they were designed as alternatives to.

For example, GNVQ units were originally broken up into separate 'performance criteria' with students required to complete portfolios demonstrating that each one had been met. This was designed to encourage 'independent learning.' In reality the complexity of the assessment process had the opposite affect. Students become even more dependent on their teachers and lecturers as they sought to decipher what was required of them and to help them record their independent learning in the mandatory course log books. Rather than encouraging research skills, GNVQ 'evidence gathering' requirements also resulted in the emergence of specifically designed textbooks outlining how particular evidence requirements could be met—more 'taskism.'

The amount of assessment may have been reduced. The level of assessment in the original version of GNVQ, which was likened by Ecclestone (2002) who gives a vivid account of 'delivering' them to testing every bullet in an armaments factory, was not sustainable for either teachers or students, but the competence approach itself continues to be influential. It is increasingly common on Foundation 'degrees', such as those to which teaching assistants may soon be relegated and, alarmingly, takes up most of the time of trainee teachers on 'standards-based' post-graduate teacher training.

Each of the new vocational diplomas will also include 'functional skills' in English, maths and ICT. Looking at the draft specifications, any reader with a working knowledge of post-16 education will recognise the similarities between these and the current 'key skills' which have evolved as stand-alone qualifications comprising multi-choice tests and portfolio evidence. Functional 'skills' will also be a compulsory part of GCSE syllabuses and students will not be able to gain a full GCSE without completing them.

It is possible that, as humanities, arts and modern foreign languages are already no longer compulsory under the National Curriculum, many students, particularly those at level 1 or those on the new 'work-based' learning programme, could be restricted to a core curriculum based around functional skills. A new educational underclass or third tier, destined for a life of 'McJobs', unskilled and casualised employment.

A sad conclusion

It seems the years of education and training reform that we have reviewed since 1944 have resulted only in raising the age of selection in state schools from 11-plus, briefly to 16, before falling again to 14 with preparation for the parting of the ways beginning with assessment at entry to infant school. This assessment is not unduly negative but realistic. Only by confronting with sober senses the real situation as we find it, can we propose to do anything about it. Before turning to this in our last chapter, we want to place what has gone wrong with education in England in a larger context to reinforce the seriousness of our concerns.

Chapter 5

Not a learning but a certified society

In many ways humanity stands at a crossroads. According to the government's own 2007 Stern Review there may be as little as a decade to transform the rapacious capitalism that has been globalised to the whole planet before runaway and irreversible environmental changes set in. Certainly, the rising generations now at school, college and university face an uncertain future in the world that has been created for them. It is tragic that just at the point in history when in the interest of human survival social control has to be reasserted over the economy, the possibility of even attempting to do so has been abandoned by triumphalist free-market fundamentalism. Education at all levels has played a large part in enabling and celebrating this new millenarianism while increasingly closing off any alternatives to it. In place of 'a learning society'—so-called—this is an ecocidally insane society. And the increasingly all-embracing education and training system has, we have argued, been used to control opposition to the growing dysfunctions of the new market-state and its free-market economy. This has gone a long way to turn education into its opposite, closing down instead of opening up alternatives, so that *education* really does *make you fick, innit?*

The failure of vocationalism

New Labour have returned to the 'pathways' approach of Ron Dearing and the Tories. They rejected the Tomlinson proposals for the reform of 14-19 learning which would have constituted a small step towards achieving parity between vocational and academic learning for students in the later years of secondary school. Instead of this 'Scottish Road to Curricular Reform' (see chapter four), they reverted to the pre-comprehensive notion that different types of learning and different types of school should be offered to different groups of students/ different classes of pre-existing minds/Platonic men of gold, silver and bronze. New Labour tried to promote this as a 'post-comprehensive' initiative, a step towards increasing student choice and a further example of the move towards 'personalised learning' that is required in a postmodern society where everything is individualised. Instead, we should see it as a return to the educational apartheid of the tripartite era.

New Labour's arguments were always contradictory. As we have already instanced, in an increasingly uncertain future when, as government argued, people are likely to have a number of completely different 'careers' during their lives, why would anybody want to lock themselves into one narrow vocational pathway at the beginning of Year 10, as is now proposed? Let alone have specialist secondary schooling from an even earlier age. Surely, providing high levels of general education for everybody would be more appropriate.

The only reason for the rigidity of offering fourteen different 'practical' diplomas to the perhaps half of all pupils not progressing to academic higher education would appear to be the bureaucratic one that at the time of setting them up employers were represented by fourteen different Sector Skills Councils (now twenty five)! But even in the unlikely case employers are going to find the time to be more involved in designing the contents of the new diplomas, predictably the qualifications will still be classroom-based, like the former-GNVQs that supplemented the work-based NVQs. For example, the 10-day work placement requirements for each diploma are little different to what many students do now as 'work experience' in either year 10 or 11. There is also no guarantee that students will want to transfer to college, or to other schools, for part of the week, or that schools, realising students will take valuable resources with them, will want them to go. The local provider partnerships that government visualise, like previous 'partnerships', are therefore likely to be undermined by the need for individual institutions to survive in the market place. According to the *TES*, (13 October 2006) many schools might try conveniently to 'forget' the diplomas!

Given the absence of practical relevance, the main problem for vocational qualifications continues to be their lack of currency. Things have not moved on enough from the 1970s when American sociologist Randall Collins in his study of the rise of *The Credential Society* argued that, because of their low status, having vocational rather than academic qualifications was a major disadvantage. As an instance, many students use Advanced GNVQs to secure places in higher education but, as was the case for the inner London students featured in the last chapter, these have been at the new (post 1992) universities, not the Russell Group which rarely recognise GNVQs as entry qualifications—certainly not for prestigious courses. This is typical of how vocational qualifications, despite their various name changes, have been unable to dislodge A-levels as the main qualification for entry into higher education.

Another feature of vocational qualifications is that in their efforts to improve their standing, like 'vocational' institutions, they often drift academically. For example, as chapter four argued, under pressure to become more rigorous, GNVQs evolved into 'Vocational' and then 'Applied' A-levels and GCSEs, mimicking the academic characteristics of these qualifications but thereby alienating the very students they were originally designed for—those turned off by 'academic' learning. As a consequence, many schools and colleges reverted to the BTEC National qualifications that GNVQ had sought to replace. Introducing new specialist diplomas will not resolve the contradictions of vocationalism, only heighten them. In fact, the recent expansion of full-time vocational education in schools can be seen as part of a new strategy of social control. It is an attempt to create and sustain a new 'technical' stream of students, officially equal, but in reality, separate and unequal to those on academic courses.

Fundamentally, it has to be recognised that most employers—despite all their protestations—don't really value 'vocational skills' that much. Employers have characteristically applied new technology to automate routine tasks so that fewer workers are required in place of the less skilled they displace. As we have outlined, this has polarised the workforce. At one pole, one in three jobs today require no certification at all. One in five of people with qualifications report their qualification was not a requirement of their current employment. This includes three out of ten graduates who are forced to take 'non-graduate jobs', displacing less qualified employees. Half of all jobs in any case require less than three months' training and a quarter no more than two years (Felstead et al. 2002). At the other pole, oversupply of qualified jobseekers require raised entry hurdles to screen applicants. Élite universities also demand new academic tests for entry. Still more expensive postgraduate qualifications become necessary to progress further and a whole industry of assessment centres sorts out candidates for employment in top City firms and other multinationals, consultancies and accountancies etc. (see Brown et al., 2004). The result is rampant diploma devaluation/qualification inflation for core jobs, combined with an uncertified periphery and a disappearing middle 'hollowing out the skills base' in 'the hour-glass society.'

6.4 million people are qualified to the equivalent of NVQ level 3, but only 4 million jobs demand this level of highest qualification. Repeated efforts to shore up the 'higher technical' middle have failed. Until recently foundation 'degrees' have only staggered along by replacing declining demand for Higher

National Diplomas. Modern Apprenticeships are also mainly delivered in further education colleges and in what is left of the despised public services. Not in the vaunted private sector that is supposed to require them and be leading in building a 'work-based route' through diplomas up to Foundation 'degrees'. Despite their perpetual 'moaning' about supposed 'skills shortages' for the past forty years, this situation suits employers very well as they are oversupplied with a surfeit of certified if not qualified labour. This underpins the recent so-called 'economic miracle' in the U.S.A. and Britain, which combines high productivity growth with low wage inflation through continuous downsizing, outsourcing and immigration—'a Brazilianised' economy as the U.S.A. has been called. As the core contracts, middle managers and other professionals are delayered and deskilled along with remaining craft workers.

'Dumbing down'

One of the solutions advanced by successive governments is to make the workforce switch flexibly from one job to another as competitiveness demands. Flexibility requires so-called 'personal and transferable skills for employability'. These 'key skills', as Sir Ron Dearing called them in 1996—or 'core skills' in the Tomlinson Report (now 'functional skills' in the diplomas)—can supposedly be 'transferred' from one employment to another. Yet they are not personal, not transferable and not skills! Nor, of course, does their acquisition necessarily guarantee employment. They are generic or universal competences, required in a variety of jobs rendered increasingly similar by the use of new technology and work reorganisation. So an emphasis on 'skills' is essentially ambiguous. It represents up-skilling, re-skilling and multi-skilling for some, combined with de-skilling to semi-skilled working for many more.

In the remaining jobs that school leavers would previously have taken, demarcations between formerly discrete tasks are broken down and re-aggregated as multi-skilled occupations by integrating routine sub-tasks (and previous employees' jobs) into them. Redesignated as also requiring so-called 'personal and transferable skills', they can be filled by graduate level employees, also displaced from their previous prospective employment elsewhere.

For those who are not relegated to the vocational route, widening participation to higher education is presented as the professionalisation of the proletariat while masking an actual proletarianisation of the professions. Fifty per cent of young people may eventually enjoy 'some experience of higher education', but it is hardly higher education as we know it. Neglect of learning is reducing much of higher education to the level of training. Unlike the generalised knowledge formerly imparted by higher education, if in an obscure and academic form, and by the equivalent tacit knowledge of skilled craftwork, the new generic competences, and the bits of information that are their counterpart on 'bite-size' training packages, do not lead on to overall understanding of the purposes to which they are put. It is this closure of knowledge and skill in employment that is the motor driving the deskilling and 'dumbing down' of institutional learning at all levels.

This is not to ignore the contribution that the official learning system of education and training also makes to foreclosing the horizons of its pupils/students to which we have drawn attention in this book. When there are primary schools in which teachers seat children at different tables according to their various 'learning styles', or rearrange them into higher, middle and lower achieving groups on the basis of equally spurious psychometric 'IQ' tests, while engaging in pseudo-scientific 'brain gym' exercises for 'the right and left brain', it is obvious teachers are also affected. This is not surprising given what has happened to teacher training! But it is not to ignore also the space that still remains at different levels of learning for engagement of learners and teachers in critical thought to which we come in our last chapter. *Teaching as a Subversive Activity*, to use the title of Postman and Weingartner's 1969 book, is still possible but it is very much swimming against a still rising tide.

In particular, the decline in public debate with New Labour and Tory depoliticisation of Party politics has, in a self-defeating process that renders politicians powerless, handed policy decision to the market. We have already noted New Labour leadership's lack of concern over local election losses, since Tory and other councils often push through free-market reforms more enthusiastically than Labour ones. Similarly, the Blair government relied on Conservative votes to get the 2006 Education and Inspections Act through the House of Commons. It may be though that New Labour cannot escape politics completely and that this trick can be pulled off by Mr. Cameron's Conservatives.

Then what substance there was to New Labour's record would be lost (as it would be predictably but perhaps a little more slowly if they won). This substance was estimated in an authoritative account by Hills and Stewart to assess how far by 2005 New Labour had met their goals of ending pensioner and child poverty, together with Gordon Brown's tax credits to the working poor and 'employment opportunity for all', as well as in tackling health, education and ethnic inequalities, neighbourhood renewal and other areas of deprivation. In contrast with the preceding Conservative governments when under Mrs. Thatcher 'average living standards grew, but income inequality widened rapidly' and 'During the Major years [when] the growth in inequality was partly reversed ...'

> 'After 1997, all income groups enjoyed quite rapid growth in living standards. This did not mean much fall in *inequality*, and only a slow decline in relative poverty, but it did involve much faster growth in living standards for the poor ... and so resulted in rapid falls in absolute poverty.'
>
> (pp 325 et seq.)

Insofar as this would be sustained under New Labour government, it would be lost under the Conservatives but both so increasingly share the same premises at the centre of British politics that in England there is little to choose between them.

Politics is depoliticised by farming out decisions to arms-length agencies or quangos, as in Gordon Brown's autumn 2006 Labour Party Conference proposals for the NHS and local government. Teachers and lecturers know all too well what his 'devolution to the front line of delivery' means—more responsibility while power contracts to the centre! But since there is no alternative, there is no point in debate. Criticism is therefore 'not constructive.'

These attitudes are endorsed by mass media owned by or linked to the same corporations (often US-based) that benefit from the deskilling and foreclosure of knowledge described above. They whip up mass emotions for 'football worship', whilst reason is relinquished in events such as the public reaction to the death of Princess Diana—this before the hysteria of the so-called 'war on terror.' No wonder that fascist parties make new inroads in former Labour heartlands encouraged by widespread moods of fear and nostalgia.

The triumph of élitism

For the really rich and powerful at the top of the class structure, educational qualifications remain less important than other aspects of social capital in guaranteeing the future earning power of their offspring. This is not to imply that they will not happily pay the £20,000 or more per year required to secure a place at a leading independent ('public') school, or thereafter to attend a prestigious and lengthy course at an élite university. This is what Ken Roberts, Professor of Sociology at Liverpool University, calls 'the clearest of all class divisions' that 'splits the population into a tiny minority (less than one per cent) on one side, and the great mass of the people on the other.' The ruling class is the best organised and most class conscious of all the classes, Ken adds.

'There is no fence', he continues, between this upper class and those managers and professionals who accept 'a service relationship' to them as they join the élite's aristocratically encrusted and celebrity strewn social calendar. They are the next rung on the ladder and can be seen as constituting an 'upper middle', or what some sociologists call a 'service class' as they have taken over top management positions across society. For them education for their children remains a significant positional good, meaning they will continue to rely on the independent sector or better state schools to ensure their privileged position is maintained. These 'consumers of learning services', include better off members of the self-employed and others able and prepared to 'put their children first.' They will welcome the cut-price crammers that Sunny Varkey's Dubai-based GEM group with its advisory board chaired by Sir Mike Tomlinson and other opportunists, like Chris Woodhead's company Cognita, are hoping to get public funding for under the 2006 Act.

Previously, New Labour feared that this section of 'the middle class' might opt out of the welfare state altogether, leaving a rump of council schools and charity hospitals. The government aimed many of their policies at keeping them on board, through 'gifted and talented' streams in schools, for instance. But now that they are closer to privatising completely what is left of the welfare state, New Labour or their Conservative successors may be tempted to hasten the process with vouchers (as in nurseries and further education), possibly building on Gordon Brown's 'baby bonds' that parents are meant to save for their newborn's higher education.

In many parts of inner-London and other cities where the very rich and the very poor live cheek by jowl (Bristol with its ring of private schools, for example), an existing hierarchy of schools with increasingly complicated admissions procedures will be accentuated by Academies and 'trusts.' This will allow schools to 'choose' students even more than Mrs. Thatcher's supposed 'parental choice' already allows them to do. As Stephen Ball's subtle ethnographies have shown, while making applications for 'good' state schools, many of these parents will also apply for a local independent school, being able to afford becoming part of the thirteen per cent of London parents who educate their children privately. Lesley Pugsley (2004) has demonstrated similar 'choices' being made (or not) by a range of parents and their children across the social spectrum in South Wales.

As these studies and others show, as more and more young people increasingly rely on education as the main vehicle for occupational placement, a potential problem for élite schools is how to continually differentiate themselves from those considered their inferiors. This becomes still more an issue when established qualifications, like GCE A-level, no longer serve as qualifications for only a small minority but have instead become a 'mass' qualification. Indeed with 750,000 entries each year, a 96 per cent pass rate and almost 23 per cent of entries receiving an A grade, A-levels, originally designed for 5 per cent of the cohort, are no longer the 'gold standard' qualification they once were.

Élite universities, not just Oxbridge colleges, now have to turn away considerable numbers of students with top grades. Recent proposals from Oxford University to change admission procedures so as to increase the number of students from poorer backgrounds met with instant hostility from the independent sector. The High Master of St. Paul's school (Annual Fee £20, 895) told *the Guardian* (27 July 2006) that Oxford's policy was 'dangerous.' There was similar bleating about Bristol University's previous modest 'social engineering.'

Yet despite their increased popularity, there is little or no proper evidence that A-level 'standards' have fallen in the way that the critics believe. The truth of the matter was succinctly put in the *Times Higher* (18 August 2006) by Alan Ryan, Warden of New College Oxford:

'It is obviously true that A levels used to be not so much harder as more straightforwardly attuned to old-fashioned single-subjects honours degrees at traditional universities.'

And he ought to know! Nevertheless, discussion about how to make A-levels 'harder' will inevitably continue, partly because many of the traditional universities do not want to change their degree courses. Nor do academics who are too busy researching want to spend much time teaching those ill prepared for them.

We should not be surprised therefore at the future introduction of A+ or A* grades. We can also expect concerted efforts by élite schools and universities to create new forms of certification, as Medical and Law Schools at Cambridge and elsewhere have already done. According to the *TES* (19 August 2005) for example, a secret conference called by Dr. Anthony Seldon, the headmaster of Brighton College, was planned to discuss the implications of the terminal decline of the gold standard. Other private and a few of the more academic state schools already make a virtue of advertising their adoption of the International Baccalaureate, 'International' GCSEs and now the new Cambridge Pre-U qualification. Meanwhile, for the mass the obsession with spelling and mental arithmetic continues, fuelling narrow phonic approaches to reading and the chanting of times-tables in primary schools.

Should I stay or should I go?

For the majority of young people, not 'gifted' with the expensively acquired cultural capital of privileged home and private schooling, it is an increasingly fraught dilemma whether to stay on in school sixth form or further education. Or whether to leave and when in hopes of finding one of the few decent Modern Apprenticeships or other means of learning while earning. Faced with a situation where they have to achieve more and more simply to stand still on the qualifications escalator, many 16-18 year-olds drift from school to further education. If they 'drift up' the system, so much the better but many drop out.

That many students are prevented from accessing high status qualifications and are offered 'vocational alternatives' instead, casts doubts on whether the higher levels of participation in education which were a feature of the 1990s will be sustainable. Evidence from recent years already shows that while more students stay on, the rate of increase has slowed. According to DfES figures, while participation in full-time education after 16 increased from 51.5 per cent to 69.3 per cent in the ten years till 1997, it was still only 72.8 per cent by 2002 and 73.8 per cent by 2004. Participation by 17-year-olds, standing at 58.2 per cent in 1998 had reached 59.1 per cent by the end of 2002 and reached 60.1 per cent by 2004.

The raising of university fees did not result in the anticipated dramatic decline in applications, save from adult, working-class and some minority ethnic group students. The original target of fifty per cent of 18-30 year-olds enjoying 'some experience of higher education' by 2010 could never be met though. It was successively rowed back from by government, being finally abandoned in 2006 by Alan Johnson. The latest figures show 42 per cent of 17-30s in full-time higher education in England (37.3 of males and 46.8 of females), down 1.4 per cent from the 2002-3 peak.

If figures for training are included then the percentage in institutionalised learning of all sorts is higher—the DfES claims over 80 per cent of 16 year-olds staying on. However, a 2003 Learning and Skills Council report argues that securing participation beyond current levels will be difficult. This is not only because of the demographic decline that will also affect higher education recruitment. The report confirms that increases in participation were helped by the introduction of GCSEs in 1988 and do not represent the continuation of a 'generational shift' towards staying on. What is equally significant from the report is the increase in the levels of qualifications that young people now have with well over fifty per cent of 19 year-olds having a level 3 certificate, the equivalent of GCE A-level. As we have pointed out, this supply is not matched by the level of employer demand for those with this level of qualification.

The implications of what we have already referred to as qualification inflation or diploma devaluation are swiftly becoming apparent in relation to graduate employment. While statistics continue to show that the earning returns from having a degree continue to be much higher than the returns from level 3 qualifications such as A-level, it is also the case that as the number of graduates grows and as employers have more opportunities to recruit them, then the less opportunities there are for non-graduates. According to Professor John Bynner and his colleagues in a 2003 Report for HEFCE, Britain's graduate labour market is already overcrowded. As we have recorded, many are forced to take 'non-graduate jobs', displacing others.

The benefits of continuing to university will increasingly be measured in terms of the costs involved, particular in tuition fees, where from September 2006, instead of a flat rate of originally £1,000, universities have been able to charge up to £3,000. In future, despite government assurances to the contrary, it is more or less accepted by all involved that, as long as there is not too much perturbation in the system during the interim period that the government clearly regards as experimental, fees will rise again in 2010 and perhaps be uncapped altogether. This is obvious even to the Vice-Chancellors who nearly all pretended there was no market by all charging the same maximum fee allowed. Clever though they thought this was, they also know that they cannot sustain this where fees rise to the £18,000 Oxford already needs to cover its annual average undergraduate teaching costs. Even with a restricted return of maintenance grants for the poorest and even if students do not have to start repaying their loans until they hit a minimal level of earnings, it is likely that with the average student debt amounting to over £20,000, prospective entrants will even more cautious before starting higher education.

A recent study by one of the authors of year twelve (lower sixth students) found that twenty seven per cent were less likely to go to university following the introduction of fees. Other studies confirm falls in the proportion of students from lower socio-economic and minority ethnic groups and in the percentage coming from state schools. Adult access students are already virtually an extinct species in higher education. For some time now, with the average student rent at about £250 per month, key divisions have emerged between students able to follow the traditional middle-class practice of 'going away' to university and those who, out of economic necessity, continue to live at home and study. One in five undergraduates are now reported as doing this, especially at former-polytechnics.

Education and social exclusion

And what of the other *Half of Our Children* not intended for higher education? These include the 2.2 million children growing up in workless households amongst the twelve million Britons still at or below poverty level, despite Gordon Brown's working families tax credits for the deserving poor. For the still aspiring respectable or 'ordinary' kids and their parents in the working-middle of society, manufactured moral panic encourages fear and loathing of the 'underclass' into which we have argued a section of the traditional manually working class have been driven. Simultaneously celebrated as *Shameless*, they are also ridiculed by the metropolitan élite who fear their drug-driven criminality.

Education and training has played a big part in constituting this 'underclass' through worthless vocational qualifications. Paradoxically, remedial efforts to overcome social exclusion often only confirm it. Teachers concern for 'boys underachievement' amongst the white working class parallel fears of a black rap culture. Once what is left of Connexions and the Youth Service after Local Authorities are cobbled together with Social Services in Children's Trusts, an attempt will be made to mentor back into the system those rejected by it. But, like U.S. ghetto 'gangstas', it is feared that the 'dumbed down' are 'chaving it' by turning their hooded heads on any sort of learning.

Those most in danger of social exclusion will therefore be central to New Labour's 'relentless focus on the basics.' They will be sent to college at 14, though not all will arrive there. This is the ungrateful nemesis of New Labour's educational effort. Drilled by a narrow and repetitive inculcation of literacy, numeracy, phonics, facts, figures and SATs, many of these children anticipate from earlier and earlier ages a worthless and workless future. 'I think I'll be a zero miss', one little girl taking her first SATs foretold her future to an educational researcher (Reay and Wiliam 1999).

What the Blair/Brown governments never realised was that education and training cannot work in limbo. They have to prepare for a viable future where what is learnt can be applied. Too many vocational routes are dead ends. Meanwhile everybody also knows that academic disciplines, supposedly untainted by practical application, actually lead to the glittering prizes. University students certainly know it. Snobbery and racism raddles the whole hierarchy of competing higher education institutions.

Increasing numbers of other young people know this too and react against it from earlier ages. They are the downside of the economic miracle that has maintained a decade of 'full employability' by combining job insecurity for those who are employed with a periphery of part-time, temporary, contract workers, ducking and diving at two or three part-time and temporary jobs at once for as long as they can and fiddling and thieving when they can't. This is the society New Labour inherited and has sustained. It is one that will be driven further by *Personalisation through Participation* (DfES 2006) with reversion to tripartite type: academies and sixth-form A-level factories for the 'gifted and talented', followed by specialist schools and technical colleges, with that relentless focus on the basics for those who end up in Non-Advanced further education. The result in terms of educational haves and have nots is scrawled on a university toilet wall: 'Go and get a job you student ponces' and underneath in another hand, 'Like I should care what a bog cleaner thinks?'

'Education make you fick, innit?'

This seems to be a gathering opinion as disillusion with 'learning' goes far beyond the dreaded 'Status 0' NEETs, the ten per cent of 17-year-olds identified in the 2005 *14-19* White Paper as 'Not in Employment, Education or Training.' Disillusion is now widespread even amongst those with professional self-interest in providing 'learning services' at schools, colleges and universities. Creeping credentialism has soured their relations with those they teach. The old slogans have worn thin since the Confederation of British Industry declared 'a Training Revolution to turn Britain into a Learning Society' by 2000. Then New Labour's millennial enthusiasm for education had the No. 10 Delivery Unit's Michael Barber (now departed to private management consultancy) urging teachers to recall 'ten new things you have learnt' at the end of every day!

Such naïve views of 'learning' as self-evidently good ignored the obvious that what is learnt can be irrelevant, false or morally wrong. Prisons are very good schools of crime for instance. The learnings of lunatics, flat-earthers and other more harmful prejudices and delusions are also learnt, often laboriously, from the studious interpretation of teachings and texts. 'Masterminds' and the University Challenged recall disconnected bits of information under pressure. Exam techniques are expensively honed to confuse knowledge with its presentation in acceptable literary form. Ever more selective higher education sifts the first-class from second-and third-rate minds and, as selection penetrates the entire school system, primary and secondary teachers differentiate their classes into the HAPs, MAPs and LAPs (higher, middle and lower achieving pupils). Psychometricians claim to calibrate the differences and 'IQ' is back with a vengeance but with no more scientific justification than it ever had.

New theories assign 'learning styles' and 'multiple intelligences' to the differentiated. Ancient prejudices live on in combination with the latest genetic predictions and other snake oil solutions. Learning is 'personalised' so that individuals negotiate their own learning plans through the seamless web of learning provision. This is a different but equal apartheid where 'tactile learners' with 'practical intelligence' are matched to the vocational routes that suit them best while the 'linguistic and logical' are accelerated towards higher education. Meanwhile, schools select by ability in their specialisms.

It is easy for teachers to fall in with these old habits but in all the talk about 'learning', what is being talked about is lost. Information is confused with knowledge, behavioural competence with holistic skill and learning at all levels with its assessment. What is clear to the growing number of disillusioned is that in important respects society is not learning at all but becoming more ignorant. It is not just that teaching to tests may not, after all, have improved literacy and numeracy when student standards of spelling and maths are slipping but, more importantly, corporately owned mass media daily plumb new depths of banality and sensation.

Once considered to be a right or a privilege, education has become a commodity. As privatisation and competition proceeds apace, what sort of education you get increasingly depends on what you can afford. Many students already only consider the 'exchange value' to be gained from continuing in education. Rather than being judged in terms of its intellectual benefits, succeeding in education has become more about negotiating an obstacle course. Rather than producing a learning culture, a 'culture of instrumentalism' predominates where students only learn what they need to, when they need to. Worse still, the pressures of league tables, which now apply to universities and departments within them as well as to schools, mean that teachers only teach what they need to. For example, a *Times Educational Supplement* front page declared 'No need to read books' (13 October 2006) providing examples of English teachers teaching 'extracts' rather than encouraging students to read whole books, so as to maximise their chances at GCSE.

The mass of students and trainees working their way through this certification system get less and less for more debt and more effort. Slaving at 'McJobs', they pay more for courses reduced towards 'bite-sized chunks'. So further and higher education students move from one module to another with no established peer groups and sensing that no one cares about them in increasingly chaotic and overcrowded institutions where they either sink or swim. They have little time and space for generalised reflection and negotiation of meaning with their teachers. Even on the most traditionally academic courses in élite universities which can be expected to raise their fees the highest as soon as they are permitted to do so, anecdotal evidence indicates students are churning out essays and other assignments as a mark of quality over competitors. But most students are well aware the required formats do not demonstrate real knowledge, or even thought, on their part but are a matter of acquired technique.

A multi-million pound internet industry now enables students to purchase finished essays and assignments that have been written for them by 'specialists'. The repeated accusations of plagiarism—and of falsification all the way from reports of primary headteachers fiddling their SAT returns to secondary and higher education students buying and selling exam course work—is further confirmation that 'ends' have become more important than the means and that an increasing number of students now no longer consider it necessary to learn at all. As a result, government have implemented a culling of course work from GCSE (for a long time regarded as a cornerstone of progressivism) and a return to traditional examinations throughout the system to stop 'internet cheats'. However, it is unlikely this will stop students, their parents or even some of their teachers from adopting desperate measures to ensure they, their children or their schools stay on the standards juggernaut and are not identified as 'strugglers'.

Parents are increasingly 'interested' in education in that they are often prepared to use all means possible to get their children into what they consider to be 'good schools'—private coaching, moving house, even regularly attending church on Sunday for a year or two! Yet at the same time they invariably show little desire to become involved in day-to-day decision making, for example by becoming school governors or even attending school AGMs. For many teachers meanwhile, 'teaching' continues to be a daily grind, an endless succession of 'what to do on

Monday morning'; in schools an activity restricted by 'behaviour problems'; in colleges and universities by endless administration. And everywhere, the constant pressure to meet bureaucratic targets. 'A system driven by anxiety', as the Archbishop of Canterbury commented.

Does it have to be this way? Unlike right wing critics who argue that the only way to restore education as an intellectual activity is to restore its exclusiveness and limit participation, this book concerns itself with the need for popular and democratic alternatives and argues that there continue to be grounds for optimism. It is to these that we turn in our last chapter.

Chapter 6

Putting it back together—How we can reform education for the 21st century?

A new approach to teaching and learning

At the centre of an alternative education strategy there will need to be a new consensus about teaching and learning. Chapters four and five have described how learning has been warped to become primarily an instrumental activity. For many school teachers, the success and effectiveness of their careers is judged in terms of how well their students do in an array of tests and exams. In colleges it has long been the case that if your courses do not attract funding they close. Now 'non-viable' departments in universities and whole universities and colleges are threatened with closure or merger if they are not competitive enough to attract fee-paying students, government research funding and private investment for 'spin-off' enterprise. This is not to imply that teachers are no longer interested in exploring the wider aspects of teaching and learning, or their own enthusiasms and research interests; merely to argue that as the pressures on teachers at all levels of the system tighten and as pay and promotion become increasingly determined by crude indicators of student progress in competition with other schools, colleges and universities, other more inspirational reasons for entering teaching and undertaking research and scholarship, have taken a back seat.

For students also, relationships with school, college and university have become increasingly pragmatic, or 'positional'—viewed only in terms of the material advantages they may lead to. Once again this does not imply that the culture of education has, or can be, completely reduced to that of a shopping mall, as Wes Shumar has described U.S. universities. But neither does it assume that before the watershed 1988 Education Reform and 1992 Further and Higher Education Acts education was an unquestionably enjoyable experience for all those involved. Chapter two identified the weaknesses and limitations of the 1944 Act as well as what went wrong subsequently in chapters three and four. Yet the market-based, certified—if not certifiable—society described in chapter five, which our education institutions now serve distorts the nature of learning and vastly restricts its potential while closing off any apparent alternatives.

The contention of this book is that it is still possible to reshape education at all levels and to transform it into more than just 'schooling.' While it does not seek to provide definitive policies for the future, it attempts to address the general principles on which we can move forward.

Should learning be valued for its own sake?

On what principles should an alternative approach to the curriculum be constructed? Teaching and learning in England has been dominated by what has been referred to as the 'liberal humanist' approach. In this tradition, learning is considered an intrinsic activity, something that should be valued for its own sake. Accompanying this is the belief that education should be a 'neutral' activity, justified because it allows a process of self development rather than being pursued for material gain. Liberal humanism also emphasises the significance of self-expression, creativity and, of course, 'freedom' of thought.

But liberal humanism also makes other, rather more controversial assumptions. According to Richard Peters and Paul Hirst, whose ideas, while not original, were highly influential in the new college and university education departments of the 1960s and 1970s, the different subject areas of knowledge should be regarded as exclusive of one another. They have their own forms, rules and conceptual tools which anyone who wants to pursue research or scholarship within a particular field must first equip themselves with. As well as divisions of knowledge, the liberal academic tradition also assumes hierarchies of knowledge. For example, it has tended to disregard 'vocational' learning and, in England in particular, has considered the arts and humanities superior to the technical and the applied. The hierarchies associated with the liberal humanist approach to learning, while continuing to provide the backbone of traditional universities, also justified the ethos behind the grammar and sixth form curriculum post-1944.

Recently, the sociologist Frank Furedi has tried to reaffirm the value of the liberal tradition. At first reading many of Furedi's arguments appear convincing and find an echo amongst academics in pursuit of knowledge for its own sake, as they think of it. For example, he argues that intellectualism has been marginalised at the expense of commodification and commercialism and 'education for its own sake' has been replaced by an instrumentalism which views the acquisition of knowledge purely as a technical process. This has resulted in a new philistinism. To an extent we agree with him but while Furedi distances himself from those who claim that extending educational opportunity beyond relatively basic provision will inevitably lead to falling standards and 'dumbing down', he is anxious to defend traditional conceptions of culture from what he regards as the anarchy of 'relativism'. This is the view that knowledge, morals and values can never be absolute, but only relative to the individuals or groups who hold them.

Furedi alerts us to the continued dangers of 'post-modern' relativism with its replacement of more general theories of the world by a fragmented and 'deconstructed' conception of knowledge. The problem is that his defence of liberal humanism is selective. In particular, ironically for a sociologist, he sidesteps sociological investigations such as those of Pierre Bourdieu in France. They went below the surface justification of education and research for their own sake to show how this ideology of education, as Ron Barnett called it in relation to higher education in this country in 2003, serves to reproduce the selection of an élite. We have argued that the raising of student fees, especially if or when they are uncapped in a free market, will make this much more obvious because only the rich will be able to afford longer and more expensive courses.

For many of its critics, liberal humanist approaches have not only been used to maintain traditional subject boundaries, but also academic hierarchies where the pursuit of knowledge is restricted to scientists and researchers in the 'academic community'. Here there is always a clear division between researchers and teachers who are regarded as a lower form of life. This is encouraged by the current competitive Research Assessment Exercise in higher education. This turns liberal humanist enthusiasm for free thinking into individual academic careerism, while alternative conceptions of knowledge generalised beyond traditional disciplines are lost. Instead of 'knowledge for its own sake' it is necessary to raise the old question of what is useful knowledge; not just for the vocational aspirations of students and the needs of employers but for what is really useful to society as a whole.

As chapter two emphasised, the move towards comprehensive education in the 1960s and 1970s did not bring such a new approach to the school curriculum. Forced on the defensive by those who sought to defend selection and privilege, many of the more academically successful comprehensives incorporated much of the grammar school tradition. As a result, from the introduction of comprehensive schools to the imposition of the National Curriculum, challenges to current definitions of what should be learned and how the curriculum should be organised have remained marginal. Similarly, further education and the polytechnics lost their often brave attempts to combine theoretical with practical learning as they drifted towards the academic ideal or were relegated to limited and competence-based forms of vocational training. The next section of this chapter examines some of these alternative practices and considers whether they can form the basis of a new approach to learning.

Classroom progressivism

Chapter two referred briefly to the progressive classroom practice of the 1970s. In emphasising the importance of self-development and encouraging creative expression, especially in the primary schools, the progressive education of the 1970s was influenced by the spirit of liberal humanism. But in challenging the status of the 'official' curriculum, progressive teachers were also implicitly critical of the underlying philosophical and pedagogic assumptions of liberal humanism. For example, they emphasised the equal importance of the 'unofficial' knowledge that students brought with them from their communities. In curriculum areas like humanities, they also argued for a new interdisciplinary approach similar to some of the new universities at the time where many of the new graduate entries to the profession had studied. Rather than providing a detailed syllabus, the interdisciplinary courses which emerged, initially in the form of teacher assessed CSE Mode 3 schemes, were often frameworks. They were constructed around themes on which individual schools were able to develop their own courses. This paralleled well established primary school project work as well as radical experiments in independent undergraduate study at the Polytechnic of East London for example (see Robbins 1988).

These new courses provided secondary school teachers with considerable autonomy. Because of their particular focus, the new social studies, world women's and peace studies, courses in schools also assumed the potential to challenge official conceptions of knowledge still further. Particularly when some practitioners brought with them their own radical political credentials allied to a growing labour movement and supported by parents (support that was later lost). The new sociology of education also referred to in chapter two sought to explore the politics behind the official curriculum. It argued that all knowledge was interest bound and that official knowledge was the product of established power structures in society. For example, subjects like English which were supposed to encourage creativity and imagination instead reflected an inert 'high culture' that reinforced an élitist view of the world.

Can the progressivism of the 1960s and 1970s form the basis of a new kind of learning? The weaknesses and the contradictions of classroom progressivism have been reviewed in detail elsewhere (Jones 1983) but some of the issues can be addressed briefly here. Though many of the new curriculum initiatives were the products of a variety of teacher networks or working groups and the enthusiasm and the commitment of the classroom progressives cannot be disputed, the understanding and support of those not directly involved in the profession could not be assumed. With some exceptions, the potentially liberating pedagogy of the classroom was not promoted outside school amongst parents and in local communities. Progressive education remained essentially a 'professional' activity initiated and controlled by teachers in the classroom, rather than being the product of a wider popular agenda. The same can be said of the critiques made by academic radicals which tended to collapse in on themselves, isolated on university campuses.

We should not deny the importance of continuing to promote alternative forms of practice for teachers in schools, colleges and universities. The U.S. magazine *Rethinking Schools* (www.rethinkingschools.com) is an excellent example of how radical and progressive educators can address current social and political issues through their teaching while also exchanging experiences to spread ideas. In this country, Terry Wrigley has provided examples of how teachers can successfully deal with 'controversial issues' in the classroom; how they can confront subject divisions and exploit the spaces offered even in a tightly proscribed National Curriculum in areas like 'citizenship.' In higher education similarly, where there is as yet no National Curriculum (though common lists of the 'outcomes' of different courses move in that direction), it is also important to preserve 'critical space', as one of us called it (with Canaan 2005).

But we would argue that while raising controversial issues in the classroom will always be an essential part of an alternative curriculum, radical teaching by itself is not enough. 'Curriculum socialists', whether in schools, universities or what is left of general studies in colleges and sixth forms, underestimate the extent to which the 'normal' curriculum is the product of much wider historical practices and they also overestimate the autonomy of the institution. We return to this issue when we examine the campaigning strategies we need.

A 'new' vocationalism?

Part of the criticism that was made of academic approaches was that liberal humanism was 'irrelevant' to the concerns of the majority of people. It was conceded that everyone should have the chance to read Shakespeare for instance but what was the point if it had no connection with the rest of their lives? In

England, until comparatively recently, except in certain privileged areas such as military research, the educational establishment has been reluctant to give industry, commerce and the practical application of knowledge equal status in the curriculum. The reasons for this are complex and relate to the historical features of English culture, particularly the relationship between a selective education system and ruling institutions and élites. But the distance between education and industry was also strengthened by the autonomy enjoyed by educational professionals in the post-war period.

Considering the lack of status for vocational learning, it is surprising that one of the most significant challenges to the traditional school curriculum came from within the 'new vocationalism' of the 1980s. Even more so because, as chapter two observed, the intervention of the Manpower Service Commission in particular, especially into the school sector, served eventually to strengthen central control over schools and colleges and to introduce the new contracting forms of funding to them. But the Technical and Vocational Education Initiative (TVEI) introduced as a pilot in fourteen LEAs in 1983 proved successful enough to be extended to all schools five years later and was acclaimed by many as a progressive alternative to the conventional academic curriculum (Dale 1990), despite Sir Keith Joseph's intentions for it.

Like progressivism in primary and secondary classrooms, the general studies movement in further education and Independent Study at university, the new TVEI courses emphasised the importance of an alternative way of learning—in particular the completion of project and activity based learning, sometimes referred to as 'learning by doing.' In response to the attacks on education in the supposedly 'Great Debate', TVEI tried to address the issue of 'relevance.' Being much more general in content than the narrow technical education of the post-1944 technical schools and apprenticeship-linked further education, TVEI was justified in terms of being a response to the changing (and as it was argued, post-Fordist) needs of the workplace in relation to the potential uses of new technology rather than the restrictive 'needs of employers.'

TVEI courses emphasised practical teamworking rather than individual study for selective examination and the importance of 'knowing how' rather than the 'knowing what' of academic learning. Instead of 'book learning', learning was considered to be something developed through 'experimental' and 'problem solving' exercises with an emphasis on working collaboratively and on 'team building.' These were the qualities that employers said that they wanted in employees—and some still say it, while often contradicting themselves by their selective recruitment practices.

Compared with other highly centralised MSC initiatives, TVEI was, like the CSE mode 3 schemes referred to above, essentially a framework from which local schemes could be developed. The programmes included 'core' modules, more specialist options and allowed also for GCSE work to be included. The autonomy enjoyed by local TVEI consortiums bridging schools and colleges meant that there were a wide variety of schemes. While in some places TVEI reproduced the competence-based training criticised in earlier chapters of this book, TVEI's proponents argued that the most progressive schemes combined cross-curricula and inter-disciplinary learning with community and work-based projects for all students. They also challenged traditional gender divisions by emphasising the increased opportunities for girls, in technical areas for example.

In other words, it was argued that, despite its relationship to the MSC as the pioneering agency of what became the new market-state, teachers and lecturers were able to both subvert and 'liberalise' TVEI while preserving the practices of progressive education. TVEI courses not only contained the potential to re-engage students bored by 'irrelevant' academic study but also allowed learners to make connections between different aspects of work and community.

Yet the potential shown by TVEI courses should not be exaggerated. As Jones (1989) observed, even if some programmes included modules on 'understanding industry', they lacked any sense of understanding that things could be organised differently. In contrast, the early twentieth century U.S. educationalist John Dewey (1966, 318), argued for:

'An education which acknowledges the full intellectual and social meaning of a vocation would include instruction in the historic background of present conditions; training in dealing with material and the agencies of production; and study of economics, civics, and politics, to bring the future worker into touch with the problems of the day and the various methods proposed for its improvement. Above all, it would train the power of re-adaptation to changing conditions so that future workers would not become blindly subject to a fate imposed upon them.'

By these standards TVEI fell well short.

Still missing—a strategy for the curriculum:
what sort of knowledge do we need?

Like the classroom progressives, TVEI enthusiasts failed to confront wider relationships between curriculum, class and power. TVEI was not a national alternative programme but a series of local initiatives in which teachers and lecturers exploited both the professional space then remaining to them but also the relatively generous funding of the Manpower Services Commission.

Since the imposition of the National Curriculum on schools, progressive teachers have not been able to produce such a serious alternative. Anger has been directed at the authoritarian way that the National Curriculum was imposed and at the lack of 'professional autonomy' allowed to teachers, while hostility towards Standard Assessment Tests and the league tables for which they are designed has not abated. English teachers were often at the head of anti-SATs campaigns but in calling for an end to government interference their demands were primarily defensive. An alternative consensus about basic curriculum principles has not emerged to address not only what students should learn but also how they should learn it. Such an alternative would understand that the reinvigorating of the curriculum must be as much a political revaluation as a professional project. One that prioritises particular values and conceptions of social justice and sustainability—and as a result cannot be left to teachers and educationalists alone.

In any discussion about an alternative curriculum, there must be the recognition that knowledge is not uninterested and that all learning ultimately has a social purpose. In other words, as argued above, traditional liberal humanist assertions about learning for its own sake, must be seen as a smoke screen.

In one respect, while encompassing liberal humanist assumptions about subject independence and the importance of divisions between teachers and taught, the National Curriculum represented a departure from the 'learning for its own sake' tradition. The initial proposals for the National Curriculum expressed the intention to

'secure for all pupils in maintained schools a curriculum which equips them with the knowledge, skills and understanding that they need for adult life and employment'   (DES, 1987)

This provoked hostility from liberals and conservatives alike. However, in itself the above statement, along with the commitment to ensure a 'broad and balanced' entitlement, is largely innocuous. It implies however agreement on what knowledge is 'needed' and this cannot be separated from debate about the nature of the society in which it exists. As chapter three made clear, the National Curriculum itself was designed (reportedly by Kenneth Baker on the back of an envelope) without any debate to promote the values that underpinned traditional Conservative approaches to society.

In contrast, an NUT curriculum statement of 1990 took up the challenge laid down by the Conservative National Curriculum, declaring that the curriculum:

> '... should provide all pupils with the knowledge, skills and understanding to which they are entitled and encourage and develop attitudes which will enable then to take a full part in society ... the curriculum should aim to redress past bias and stereo-typing and present positive images of traditionally disadvantaged groups'

A pamphlet by the Socialist Movement Education Group the same year went much further in addressing the relationship between learning and established power structures. It emphasised the potentially transformative nature of an alternative curriculum that would be

> 'attentive to the real cultures of people who live in Britain. It would not transmit the versions of the national culture promoted by the dominant class. It would aim to encourage amongst students an understanding of the relationship between dominant and oppressed cultures. It would be internationalist and globally informed.'

While for the Hillcole Group of radical educationalists:

> 'Teachers should be actively engaged in opposing inequality on the basis of class, race, sex and sexuality. At the level of the formal curriculum there needs to be a fundamental reappraisal of the values and assumptions that permeate and frame the way that subjects are offered in English schools.'   (1991, 95)

These curricular alternatives have commonalities with Dewey's conception of vocational learning quoted above. They also represent a return to the perspective of early working-class radical educators, for example the Chartists and Owenites (see Flett, 2007). In response to attempts by Christian philanthropists to promote 'useful knowledge' of the Bible amongst the lower orders as part of a strategy to ensure political stability, these radical educators of the time put forward the concept of '*really* useful knowledge.' For them, really useful knowledge included an understanding of 'why people were poor.' So in the twenty-first century, as Hillcole (1997, 26) went on to argue:

'At the very least education should be an activity that exists to question the world economic system that we have so uncritically accepted as inevitable.'

Since the publication of these statements the debate about reforming the National Curriculum has been pedantic and uninspiring. As mentioned, the National Curriculum has been both pared down to the level of functional literacy and numeracy and simultaneously freighted with concerns for a limited conception of citizenship combined with consumer education, health, diet and other issues displaced by an academic approach to a narrow range of traditional subjects. Rather than being concerned with which subjects should be included and which should be left out, democratic discussion of a curriculum core could instead provide a framework that particular themes of learning should be constructed around. Rather than pursuing a (so far) fruitless strategy of attempting to improve the status of vocational learning compared with academic study, in a curriculum organised around different principles there would be no such divisions. Students could if they wish still develop practical and occupational skills within a much more holistic curriculum, together with the inquisitive approach proposed by Dewey. The best of the polytechnic alternative to selective academic higher education could be taken as a home-grown precedent, combining further practice with higher theory.

'Real personalised' learning

Discussion about an alternative curriculum will need to confront, reclaim and release the notion of 'personalised learning' from its New Labour captors. New Labour has been as anxious to promote personalised learning as they have been to promote the individualisation of other social services in the interests of consumer choice, packaged and quantified in a process of commodification. We have argued that in education this represents the latest in a series of perversions of the comprehensive ideal. Perhaps because New Labour are reluctant to abandon the slogan at least of equal opportunities, even whilst endorsing its opposite of 'opportunities to be unequal', and come out for a return to grammar schools that will necessarily fail many more than they select, New Labour has often hesitated to define what personalised learning actually means. Most recently, in the 2005 White Paper, *Higher Standards Better Schools For All*, personalised learning is the term used to describe the further differentiation of students into groups and sets, with the expansion of 'catch up' classes for those falling behind and accelerated learning for 'gifted and talented' students to race ahead.

In the current competitive and straightened economic context, personalised learning will inevitably become distorted by applications of ICT. Rather than leading to students having more control over their learning, it will become synonymous with 'teacherless learning' and the replacement of qualified teachers with computer terminals serviced by underpaid support staff. In the same way, the potential of Independent Study for undergraduates was transformed into what the National Union of Students used to call YOYO or FOFO modules (Your On Your Own so Fuck Off and Find Out!). At the same time, personalised learning will allow further differentiation of school pupils, especially as increasing numbers are sent off from 14-years-old to follow personalised learning plans at college or even in 'learning at work' for one or two days a week through the Increased Flexibility Programme—though how many of them will arrive there is another matter!

An alternative approach to the curriculum will allow us to really personalise learning for all students to develop their talents and interests. This can be aided by developing the potential for learning of new information technology, instead of restricting its use to repetitive and individualised tasks. But most of all it is a question of reducing class sizes, increasing the amount of 'one-to-one' provision and ensuring that each student has a personal tutor. So it will require considerable additional resources. Then personalised learning can ensure that learning remains an important collective and democratic activity changing the relationship between students and teachers. Though it may be that in order to maximise learning opportunities learning does not need always to be school or college based. It is essential too that schools, colleges and universities are regarded as communities of learners rather than providers of personalised customer services.

All personalised programmes of study in school and college should include some element of independent study in the sense of original discovery, creation or research with new forms of assessment and self-assessment based upon their work. (At present only art and dance/drama students are assessed mainly on their creative efforts in end of degree shows.) Investigation, experiment and debate by all students and as many other people as possible is vital today when so many received ideas are open to question. What we have called the 'critical space' within education for seeding new ideas must be preserved and extended by making scientific research, scholarship and artistic creation an integral part of the independent study of all students, rather than separating teaching from research.

This in essence is the answer to the vexed question of research in higher education which we have avoided until this point. It has become a shibboleth for many academics clinging to their status as more than teachers. Our position is the opposite—research should be generalised to as many teachers and their students as possible. This is not to deny the necessity also for specialist researchers. While opposing the concentration of all research that governments have encouraged over the past twenty years, specialised research, especially big science projects, need to be sustained through dedicated state or European research institutes. Meanwhile state-funded research should not be prostituted to commercial interests as is increasingly happening. Inevitable falsification of results and other recent scandals exemplify once again the corruption endemic to the dominance of the new market-state by profit seeking private corporations.

A new approach to funding and accountability

Discussions about learning and the curriculum inevitably lead into consideration of the funding and accountability of educational institutions. As with our discussion of the curriculum, rather than providing specific policy answers we will seek to highlight particular concerns and areas which must be addressed if a more detailed alternative is to emerge.

On the issue of school funding in particular, the response of reformers and campaigners has often remained highly general (perhaps as in our plea above for adequately funded personalised provision). Continuing to demand more funding for schools, colleges and universities while calling also for an end to fees and privatisation and the outsourcing of educational services will continue to be a key campaigning demand. If the proportion of GDP spent on education is used as a basis for comparison, then OECD statistics show that the UK barely scrapes into the top twenty. Still behind the Scandinavian countries but also France, Portugal and Belgium in spending on education, under New Labour the UK has barely reached European averages. However, as a result of the array of private sponsorship deals, grants and partnership arrangements, it is often difficult to work out exactly how much money is being spent on education. Moreover, if additional revenue goes only to consultants and private partners, as we said in the introduction, little of it percolates through to the much touted 'front-line' practitioners.

In recent years some of the most high profile campaigns have been defensive and have involved popular mobilisation in opposition to cuts and particular school closures. There has been less interest in the question of how funding has been distributed. For example, after the initial hostility to the Education Reform Act, there was little further response to the continuation of Local Management of Schools (LMS), the process where schools receive delegated budgets largely based on the size of their intakes. Or to the incorporation of further education colleges, even though this continues to pit them into cut-throat competition with one another.

The issue of institutional autonomy is an important one. Mrs. Thatcher exploited the concern that 'old Labour' LEAs were seen as bureaucratic and unable to respond to local needs. The argument behind LMS was that it would increase parental control of schools by giving more autonomy to governing bodies. The reality is that it has served as a market mechanism enabling 'popular' schools to flourish and failing schools to contract. Similarly, the market in further and—still more—higher education, where free for all competition on fee price is not far away.

If large proportions of the budget are to be delegated directly, then how can the increased social and economic differences that have emerged as a result of recent policies, be confronted? Should not these inequities rather than the number of 'bums on seats' become the main component in any new funding formula? On the other hand, can schools really enjoy 'autonomy' when they find that, in many cases, well over 90 per cent of their delegated budget has to go on staffing costs? This means they have to make decisions—about whether to employ particular teachers rather than others, for instance—on economic rather than educational grounds. Reformers often agree that schools 'should be funded according to their local needs' but then go no further. Discussion about how much autonomy individual schools should have, as well as what they should have financial responsibility for must become part of any reforming agenda.

The same goes for colleges which have become subject to close control by the Learning and Skills Council. We have suggested that the LSC's relation to the other huge post-school funding council for higher education will determine the future of further education and whether it gets absorbed by higher education (as we said, turning further education into higher education, while large parts of higher education actually turn into further education through competence-based courses, like many of the Foundation 'degrees' or post-graduate teacher training). All these contracting agencies of the new market-state will have to be replaced by a democratic reconstitution of the welfare state. It is difficult to be more specific here because once the implications of more than superficial changes to education and training are considered, these quickly entail larger changes to decentralize and democratize the state and introduce changes to local/regional government going far beyond the immediate remit of education. Such a transformation should not be confused with persistent Blair/Brown calls for 'devolved public services.'

Suffice to say here that a new approach to education funding would necessitate the end of the 'bidding culture' that has resulted in some schools, colleges and universities appearing to be awash with resources whilst others continue to crumble. We are not against private sponsors and philanthropists handing over money to be used in education, but we are opposed to them being allowed to decide which school it goes to and on what it should be spent. Most immediately, the market in higher education must be ended along with fees—replaced not by a graduate tax but by a return to progressive taxation. The hierarchy of universities competing with their various course options for fee paying students offers a model that neo-Thatcherism seeks to impose on the market in specialist schools and colleges.

A genuine debate about how educational resources should be distributed cannot be complete without a consideration of the current inequalities between different sectors of education, where it is simply assumed that the older students are—unless they are adult education students of course!—the more money should be spent on them. The assumption continues that higher education should be funded more generously than secondary which should receive more than primary and so on down to early years. 'Research' universities are also assumed to require more than those that concentrate primarily on teaching. There also remain unacceptable differences in resource levels between public and private education but discussion of these inequities and how the private sector can at least be curtailed, if not abolished, has long since fallen off most agendas. Instead, we must insist that the subsidy of private schools through charitable status should be ended, as much to end the white flight and snobbery associated with the majority of them as to redistribute resources more fairly.

Rethinking the Local Authority

As chapter two noted, local education authorities became a cornerstone of the post-war educational consensus. Replacing the old school boards, LEAs ensured that there was local democratic control over education. The chapters that followed showed how LEAs were plundered by the Conservatives and then reclaimed and remodelled by New Labour. Local Authorities, as they have now become, act as important conveyors of the standards agenda but at the same time no longer have responsibility for delivering education themselves. As 'commissioners of learning services', they have been charged with working alongside a variety of new partners. Many of the Government's 'flagship' projects, particularly the Academies programme, exclude them. Others, such as Building Schools for the Future, are presented as the only means to funding.

In some areas, especially inner city boroughs, Local Authorities are now empty shells consisting of little more than marketing teams, inspectors and health and safety advisors under a Director of Children's Services who may or may not be a former Chief Education Officer. As a result, it would be difficult to 'return' schools and certainly colleges to 'LEA control' in the way that some reformers continue to demand. Even though they have not served the interests of education, these developments force us to rethink the role of the Local Authority. We still consider that they should be at the centre of local provision, but that LEAs of the future should be different to both the post-war model and what New Labour have left us with.

Once again, reformers have not addressed this issue adequately. For example, the NUT in its 2005 *Breaking Down the Barriers* policy statement for the next five years produced in response to Government's own five-year strategy, seeks to reposition the LEA as an effective coordinator and provider of a range of school services. Yet with the exception of its support for local 'education forums' this continues to assume the continued existence of traditional 'second tier' LEAs. As Professor Peter Mortimer, former-director of the London University Institute of Education, observed, much of the NUT's policy statement 'looks back.' Discussions about the future control and accountability of schools, colleges and the role of the LEA should also look forward, but in a very different way to New Labour.

Campaigns across sectors have to be united conceptually and practically to build a national coalition of trade unions, public sector alliances, community and civil society organisations through regional and national action starting in cities such as Newcastle where there have been some successes against privatisation of council services. But Britain is in the vanguard of the marketisation of public services in Europe and so there are lessons to be learnt for and from mainland European countries. We cannot rely upon 'social Europe' as an alternative, however, whilst the Europe Union wants to liberalise the cross border supply of services to create a single market removing all barriers to private service providers making as much profit in one country as in another. This neo-liberal agenda complements the World Trade Organisation's General Agreement on Trade in Services to which we can counterpose 'GATS-free-zones.' Campaigning organisations such as the World Development Movement, Oxfam and War on Want should link their opposition to GATS in the developing world to oppose Britain's internal marketisation and privatisation programme, especially of education and health.

Urgent action to solve the admissions nightmare

Having said that we should not idealise elsewhere or the past, one area where we can learn from the more inclusive practices of other European countries as well as from our own past is on the question of school admissions. The current scramble for 'good schools' with the increasing ability of more affluent parents to either move into a school's catchment area, or to satisfy other requirements, or in the end to successfully use the appeals procedures to obtain the sought after place, is a product of the increased importance of education as a 'positional good.' Concessions obtained by opponents of the 2006 Education and Inspections Act will hardly affect all this—religious denominational schools remain outside their provisions for instance.

The competition for places, instanced in the crazy 'school runs' half way across London and other cities, is also the result of differences between schools increasing as a result of government 'diversity' agendas. If there is one issue where we are going to be prescriptive, it is in the need for an admissions policy based on 'nearest first' with statutory powers for LEAs to enforce this if necessary. In supporting the demand for a 'good local school' we are against 'bussing'—a method once used by the Inner London Education Authority to secure a social mix in some of its schools. But a proper debate and parental involvement in discussions about reducing inequalities between schools is indispensable if we are to achieve this.

The demand for a good local school can be extended not only to other education provision, such as adult and further education—including cultural and recreational facilities, but to other public services, notably hospitals, now also thrown into financial competition with one another. Caroline Benn, a lifelong lifelong educator, took the principle further and higher to argue for an entitlement of access to local universities for local students living at home, as is largely the case in France or U.S. State universities. To obviate the selection by residence that occurs with schools, she suggested that the former-polytechnics, Oxford Brookes and Anglia Ruskin, should become the local universities for Oxford and Cambridge, while the antique university colleges could become adult residential colleges to compensate all those over thirty-years-old who have been squeezed out of higher education in recent years by the 18-30-years-old fifty per cent widening participation target. At the time she was making this argument, this would have Ruskinised Oxford University instead of closing the trade union adult Ruskin College of the University as was then proposed.

School reformers, like Caroline's daughter Melissa, are unanimous in calling for the scrapping of the Academies programme, ending selection and specialist schools. However, over the issue of religious ('faith schools') division recurs. No more so than at the 2006 Annual Conference of the NUT. Delegates almost without exception remained opposed to religious schools in principle, but with disagreements about how they should be abolished, or even whether they could. The arguments are muddied by the role that churches played in compensating for the slow progress of English state education in the nineteenth century and the place of Catholic schooling in relation to the Irish and wider Catholic community, while the issue of Muslim schools cannot now be divorced from the changing situation of the Islamic community as a result of the shameful and criminal Anglo-American invasion of Iraq.

U.S. influence is also shown in New Labour's enthusiasm for 'independent' state schools which has intensified the controversies surrounding faith schools, not just Academies but also 'foundation' schools and in future the new 'trusts.' Evidence from the U.S. Charter school prototype and also from Sweden on the effects of these types of schools shows them widening social divisions but in other countries, Denmark for instance, parents have been able to successfully establish their own schools that have enjoyed local support and have complimented rather than undermined commitments to equality. There is also the question of schools that offer 'alternative' or libertarian education, for example those following Steiner and Montessori philosophies. Cold shouldered by LEAs, these schools, despite their radical and egalitarian perspectives, have often been driven into the private sector. Even there they have not been free from OfSTED harassment, as the successfully resisted attempt to close A. S. Niell's pioneering and experimentally democratic Summerhill School showed.

As the previous pages have argued, hierarchies in educational institutions state and private have reflected wider hierarchies and long-held assumptions about the importance of different types of knowledge. More recently, as chapter 4 noted, the professional influence of teachers was undermined as 'top down' models of management were imposed to deliver 'school improvement.' National Curriculum strategies which direct how teaching and learning should take place turn teachers into technicians. Similar tendencies are evident in further and higher education to turn teaching into training.

However, despite their collegial and public service traditions, educational institutions, particularly schools, have always been relatively undemocratic places. Non-teaching sections of the education workforce, for example, are generally excluded from decision making, even if many of them have close contact with parents and the local community. Despite the growth of sixth forms as a consequence of rising staying on rates, school students continue to have little if any collective organisational rights and school councils remain largely tokenistic. Attempts have been made to address this situation with the development of the 'student voice' initiative and the establishment of ESSA, the English School Students Association, as well as through NUS.

If issues of curriculum, funding and accountability are central to any new movement for educational reform, what form should this movement take? The next section of this chapter takes as its theme the question of agency—how we start organising for change.

Organising for change

After twenty years of regressive policy how do we even begin to turn things around? Without a new popular movement for education, both the critique offered by this book as well as any discussions about how schools, colleges and universities could be better run are likely to remain marginal. We can begin this task by revisiting the campaign against the 2006 Education Bill. Although unable to stop the Bill's main proposals from becoming law and involving only a tiny proportion of the thousands of teachers, parents, community groups and students who may be affected by the Bill's proposals, the coalition that emerged against the proposals for trust schools (outlined in chapter four) is an example of what is possible.

A Good Local School for Every Child was a conference held in March 2006 at London University's Institute of Education. It drew over three hundred participants from teacher trade unions, established campaigning organisations like the Campaign for State Education (CASE) and the Labour Party grass roots, together with concerned individuals and members of other Parliamentary and other parties. The NUT general secretary, professors of education, headteachers, education journalists and MPs addressed the conference with workshops taking place on a variety of themes. The conference ended without delegates committing themselves to further activities or backing any alternative programme but it did provide a glimpse of what could be done.

If much of the attention was focussed on the proposals for School Trusts, for the first time in many years the publicity generated by the campaign against the Education and Inspections Bill created space for more general discussion of other related educational issues. For example, how do we challenge the academic and vocational divide and how should we change the way that schools are currently funded? It showed that an alternative programme for education, capable of attracting widespread support, will have to be the product of a new alliance for change. It will need to be bigger, broader, bolder but also more probing than the campaign against the 2006 Bill.

The precedent of the comprehensive movement, referred to in chapter two, should not be underestimated. But it would be an exaggeration to say that this represented anything like the sort of mass grass roots movement we need now. Although receiving widespread support from the then nationally much stronger trades union and labour movement, the comprehensive movement was more of a powerful and influential pressure group that relied on the tireless commitment and organising skills of key individuals. The Labour government itself did little to increase popular involvement in the new schools, leaving them to LEA administrators and headteachers. At no time for example, did Labour try to promote a national debate, build a national movement, or even commission any sort of national report on comprehensives.

Similarly, the 1944 Act and the post-war, cross-party 'consensus' that emerged in its wake, while it had taken advantage of the popular demand for change following the victory against fascism worldwide, was the product of an alliance involving leading sections of the Labour Party, certain key intellectuals and a succession of general secretaries from the various teacher trade unions. These groups formed the nucleus of what is referred to as the post-war educational partnership. But although influential in terms of the direct access it enjoyed to government ministers and civil servants, the partnership was essentially one of experts, policy makers and administrators. Detached from the everyday experiences of teachers, parents but also students, it nevertheless acted on their behalf.

Campaigning then and campaigning now

During the post-war period, the key area for those involved in campaigning for education reform remained access to education. Improving 'equality' in education was seen primarily as an exercise in improving the under-representation of working-class children in grammar schools and then, as comprehensive reforms set in, challenging under-representation in higher education. Campaigners, researchers and policy makers also emphasised the under-representation of girls, ethnic minorities and others who were discriminated against. Concerns about inequality of access also fitted neatly with social democratic ideas that society should be a meritocracy—one where status should be achieved, rather than ascribed by birth or money. In otherwords, education was seen as a way of increasing individual mobility or redistributing social capital, rather than as a more general emancipation.

Issues of access and equal opportunities in education must continue to be a campaigning priority, particularly now that Labour governments are mimicking their Tory predecessors to try to justify a 'diversity' of schools. The limited concessions made over school admissions by the 2006 Education Bill allow admissions policies of Trust Schools to be open to greater scrutiny. They make it likely that there will be a long and drawn out guerrilla war against selection where some key victories against Trusts and Academies could accumulate into the 'unstoppable bandwagon' that even Mrs. Thatcher appreciated the demand for comprehensive schooling once became.

However, concentrating exclusively on access, or restricting future opposition to the 2006 legislation to the question of school admissions—at the expense of more general concerns about learning and the curriculum—risks sustaining the illusion that everything else about educational provision remains basically uncontroversial and that it can be entrusted to the experts and professionals to get on with the job. It also assumes, for example, that there is a general consensus about the importance of raising performance levels in the way that New Labour emphasised and that the only disagreement is over some of the ways they have gone about it. Also, about what is going on in further and higher education, generally assumed to be a more specialist concern.

Mass organisations, like the National Union of Teachers and the University and College Union, must question these assumptions from the centre of a new alliance. But building a new type of movement will also pose new challenges for these organisations, particularly their leaders. This is especially true for the NUT. Previously enjoying good relations with Labour politicians, but also with some post-war Conservative governments, the collapse of the post-war consensus and the imposition of the new market-state has seen a dramatic reversal in the NUT's influence. More recently the Union has been excluded still further from the corridors of power at the DfES. Because of grass roots opposition from its members, it has refused to sign up to the remodelling agenda for the education workforce referred to in chapter 4 and, as a result, is no longer considered a 'social partner.' The excommunication of the NUT has disorientated a union leadership relying on a close relationship with Labour. As well as posing significant questions about the future political direction of the NUT this also raises concerns about how it campaigns in the future, but also, with whom.

In comparison with other school teacher unions, like NATFHE in the colleges and polytechnics in relation to AUT in traditional universities, the NUT began life as a union that represented less privileged elementary school teachers rather than the better paid and more academic grammar school teachers. As well as fighting for improvements in their own conditions of employment and seeking to raise the status of elementary teachers to comparable levels to those enjoyed by their secondary counterparts, its members were also regularly involved in disputes about the inadequacies of the education they were compelled by law to deliver. In campaigns against practices like 'payment by results' and in their opposition to classes greater than sixty, these teachers sought allies across their localities. As a result, elementary teachers not only appealed to their local working-class communities for support, they were part of a working-class struggle to achieve improvements in educational provision.

However, it was the post-war expansion of state education as part of the more general period of post-war reconstruction that transformed the status of teachers into 'professionals.' As the elementary and secondary sectors were brought closer together, so were the two categories of teachers. Encouraged to work in partnership with their employees, the new LEAs, leaders of teacher organisations were also encouraged, because they were now 'professionals', to distance themselves from the labour movement. In turn, teacher union leaders were also keen to contrast the differences between teachers and other groups of workers.

This reactionary view of professionalism is portrayed by Walter Roy in his 1968 book *The Teachers' Union*. According to Roy, who was President of the NUT in the early 1970s, there was:

> 'a strong sense of professionalism amongst teachers, thousands of whom labour in schools, performing unpaid tasks, who display a sense of vocation, a desire to impart to their pupils a quest for truth and objectivity.'

Teachers used their new won status to justify their opposition to outside interference in their work. Roy saw teachers as a 'learned profession' resistant to any attempts, particularly by local councillors who were often less educated than themselves, to interfere in the business of teaching. While for NUT General Secretary Ronald Gould, addressing the 1964 Annual Conference, 'teachers knew the educational needs of their children ... While it is their professional duty to provide for these, it is the duty of others in education to listen.' As a result, within the post-war partnership it was accepted that issues of the curriculum and learning should be left to teachers. This resulted in a 'teacher knows best' approach to education reform with the curriculum regarded as a 'secret garden.'

Bringing teachers back in but no return to the 'secret garden'

The position of teachers as 'professionals' has always been a contradictory one and this is particularly the case today. Even in higher education, what one U.S. study calls

> 'the relative proletarianisation of the technical intelligentsia does not signify that they have become a new working class so long as they retain the ideology and culture of professionalism, one of whose characteristic features is to foster self-blame for failure.'

In the view of the authors,

'The pervasiveness of self-blame reveals the degree to which the self-perpetuating features of the academic system are introjected by one group of its victims.'　　(Aronowitz and DiFazio 1994, 225 and 256)

We argued above that the responsibilities entrusted to teachers at all levels were part of an ideological reconstruction of professionalism. This has continued to be undermined by the decline in levels of pay and conditions of service enjoyed by teachers in schools, colleges and universities and has resulted in a growing trade union consciousness amongst all these teachers and closer links between teacher organisations and the labour movement. The clearest example of this was the school teachers' pay campaign of the mid-1980s mentioned in chapter three, where a willingness to take industrial action at a national level and, in particular, to withdraw 'goodwill' by not participating in activities that were not contractual, symbolised a move away from the sort of narrow and complacent professionalism epitomised by Roy. It also constituted a break from key aspects of the politics of professionalism where the Union relied on the skills and personal contacts of its leaders to lobby its educational partners. Similarly, the joint higher education union action in support of their pay claim in 2006 involved a boycott of student assessment and examination.

Unlike the newly created UCU, the NUT has a long standing and effective network of left-wing activists grouped around the Socialist Teachers Alliance and the Campaign for a Democratic and Fighting Union, who in winning election as National Executive members, have continued to try and drag the Union further towards the more mainstream labour movement and to work more closely with other public sector unions in campaigns against privatisation and in defence of pension rights. Many of them cut their teeth during the national pay strikes of the 1980s, where they reinvigorated local branch activity.

However, only the crudest economistic type of Marxist analysis would argue that increased industrial militancy amongst teachers or the 'proletarianisation of professionals' will necessarily lead to teacher organisations developing popular alternative 'socialist' education programmes. It is equally problematic to assume that parents, particularly if they are faced with having to make last minute arrangements for their children in the event of industrial action, are always going to be supportive! In 2006 a number of students at different universities opposed the joint union action on pay demanding their money's worth for the debts they were incurring. Yet the industrial muscle of teacher unions is extremely important. Combined with the relatively high level of resources at their disposal, at least compared with those of any other educational campaigning body, this is the principle reason for organised teachers at all levels remaining the catalyst for more widespread struggles around what we have argued is now a unified education and training system.

The NUT is still unique amongst other classroom teacher organisations in that it continues to see the fortunes of teachers as being bound up with the fortunes of public education as a whole. UCU by contrast is split on this issue, part of higher education seeing itself as traditionally autonomous from the state. NUT shares the commitment to the public sector of further education and former-polytechnic lecturers and has as a result continued unreservedly to oppose attacks on comprehensive education by both Conservative and Labour governments. Not only was the NUT the only school teachers union to support the Institute of Education conference described earlier, it was a major instigator of it.

As a consequence, NUT remains very different to 'sectionalist' organisations like the National Association of School Masters/Union of Women Teachers (NASUWT), for example. The NASUWT has positioned itself as a militant defender of teachers' immediate interests. While it is quick to sanction action in individual schools where conditions of service are under threat and also ballots members over refusing to teach 'unruly' children, it generally keeps a low profile in educational debates and judges new initiatives largely on whether they increase the workload of its members, not on pedagogic grounds. While the NUT opposed the SATs on educational grounds, for instance, the NASUWT opposed them primarily because of the increase in teacher workload and their boycott was suspended when government agreed to bring in more external markers. By restricting itself to a narrow sectionalist agenda, the NAS continues to recruit teachers and currently claims a membership just below that of 250,000 strong NUT.

But in schools as in further and higher education, it is not simply a case of teachers' pay and conditions coming under attack. As the preceding chapters have made clear, not only has the job of teaching changed fundamentally but the control previously enjoyed by teachers in terms of what they teach and how they teach it has been continually undermined. As well as in schools, this applies also especially in further education but increasingly now at all levels of higher education. As a result of the degradation of teachers' skills and knowledge and the increased emphasis on business principles in running educational institutions, teachers in schools, colleges and universities remain 'professional' in name only.

Rather than being the 'managers of learning' in the way New Labour describes them in schools, or 'facilitators of learning' in further and higher education, teachers have become 'technicians.' In otherwords, there has been a complete reversal of the post-war relationship between teachers and learning.

This turn-around has also been accomplished in the changes inflicted on teacher training (as we noted it has now once again become). These have reinforced the emphasis on technical delivery and downplayed the significance of wider understanding for new teachers. In fact, teacher training is the prime example of a change in the relations between further and higher education. As we recalled, specialist trade colleges of teacher training were incorporated in the new schools of education established in universities and polytechnics from the 1960s. Their courses of post-graduate certification fulfilled the unions' long-standing demand for a graduate entry profession. Later, under attack for their academic 'irrelevance' by the Conservatives, they were forced to accept a standards-based training in competence dictated by the Teacher Training (sic) Agency of the DfES—renamed Training and Development Agency to cover the whole of the 'schools workforce.' In effect, this reduced this postgraduate certification to further education delivered within or by higher education. Just as successful teaching became defined as being able to meet a series of 'standards', teacher training has been reduced to acquiring a series of competencies.

'Deskilling'—reducing teachers to the technical performance of the competencies for effective delivery of centrally inscribed standards while at the same time heaping more direct demands upon them—has undermined post-war perceptions of 'professionalism.' This applies not only to teachers but to social workers and others: as we observed, medical education for doctors as well as nurses is also moving in this direction. It has also had a negative effect on teachers' self-perception as innovators and as agents of change. As well as encouraging the acceptance by teachers of spurious fish-oil solutions to differentiating children according to 'learning styles' and other panaceas that we have remarked, teachers' confidence has been sapped in their capacity to resist further impositions.

For example, a successful vote by union activists at the NUT's 2004 Annual conference in support of a boycott against SATs, although receiving clear support from a significant minority of members, was not able to produce the majority that Union rules required for the action to proceed. An argument continued to rage amongst NUT activists about the timing of the ballot (teachers were already well on the way to preparing their children for SATs when they were asked to vote) but the disappointing turn out was also a reflection of more long term changes. The acceptance of a 'sell-out' solution to their pay claim by UCU members in 2006 may be indicative of a similar malaise.

It is true that many members may have been unconvinced by the seriousness of their union's campaign. Many more have simply been ground down by over ten years of being required to 'teach to the tests' in schools or fulfil the requirements of various quality auditors and inspectors. But it is also the case that for many school teachers, particularly those who had little or no experience of teaching pre-National Curriculum, or those who have entered further education since incorporation, there has never been an inclination or opportunity to discuss alternatives. Much of the aging 'academic community' in universities meanwhile remains wrapped in nostalgia for 'the good old days.' They wait only to be pensioned off in an immanent staffing crisis that will hit higher education just as the fees market begins to bite.

Yet surveys continue to show that teachers at all levels remain committed to helping their students, dedicated to their vocation and committed to education and research. The fact that more young people are experiencing the contradictions of full-time education to later ages and stages than ever before, provides a situation where there is the greatest opportunity to change it. However, this means a new collective culture has to be rebuilt. Rather than returning to an inward looking 'secret garden' approach where teacher knows best, it means restoring teachers' confidence in their ability to become not only critical educational professionals prepared to use their skills to further the interests of the students they teach and the communities they serve but also to assume a more transformative role—remaining committed to improving the individual chances of their students, but also being part of wider discussions about the future and purpose of education, training, research and scholarship.

Social justice trade unionism

Alongside the industrial and professional functions of teacher trade unionism, the U.S. education journal *Rethinking Schools* has called for the creation of a 'social justice unionism' which views students, parents and community as essential partners in reform and is committed to bottom-up grass roots mobilisation against inequality in education. There continue to be very positive examples of this. During the national SATs boycott of 1993, NUT branches, especially in inner city areas, were able to use their resources to begin to build alliances with local parents against the tests, particularly those for 7-year-olds. More recently, there have been a number of high profile campaigns against attempts to turn schools into City Academies. These have invariably been led by local NUT activists and have often followed votes for strike action by Union members concerned about the effect of academies on the quality of local education. In the current divisive educational climate, however, many campaigns—even those against academies and SATs—are in danger of remaining localised unless there is effective central coordination. Only organisations like the National Union of Teachers are able to take the lead in this. That is why this chapter has concentrated on them. Union density of membership is also much higher in schools than in colleges and universities.

But to be effective, schools campaigns need to overcome the isolation of their primary and secondary sectors from each other and from the rest of the system of education and training. In Scotland, the Educational Institute unites teachers from primary to postgraduate schools. Members there cannot fall back on blaming the schools for the failings of the selective and academic system that sections of higher education have been instrumental in imposing upon schools. Nor can school teachers accept as unchangingly wonderful a mass higher education that is no longer what it was when many of them went to college or university. The system of education and training has to be comprehended as a whole by those within it who seek to change it, both teachers and taught.

This process of reconceptualising and repositioning also requires more basic changes in the public profile of education unions to complement their standing in the workplace. A small step in the right direction could, for example, be creation of trade union sponsored education information and advice centres in local high streets. As well as providing individual advice to parents, would-be students and trainees, they could also be used to organise local forums and promote discussion about issues where New Labour continue to make the running. Yet if they are to occupy a pivotal role in a new alliance for progressive change, the NUT and UCU have to ensure that their own members in direct contact with pupils and students are able to articulate and promote discussion about the need for alternatives.

Changing education, changing society

Despite the daily more apparent need for radical change to education as to other areas of a violently self-destructive society, effecting change will not be easy. The mobilising of popular support for an alternative policy is essential. But in itself this does not guarantee that such a programme will be successful, or over what time span. Finally, if radical change in education depends on the formulation of popular alternative programmes, their existence still leaves teachers and lecturers to deal with Willis' 'Monday morning problem' referred to in our introduction. For Willis, practitioners wanting to fight for an alternative could not contract out of the messy business of sorting out the day-to-day problems of their students.

Even if as educators we have severe reservations about the sort of education available to young people in this country at the beginning of the twenty-first century, it would be farcical if as practitioners we did not do our best to make sure that our students are able to fulfil their own personal aspirations as far as possible. Unlike many right wing critics, we welcome the expansion of higher education and that more and more students are gaining their GCSEs. We welcome more positive relationships between teachers and students but also between teachers and parents as a precondition for more prolonged debate about the future of education.

A first step might be to establish for as many people as possible the normality and desirability of full-time education to 18. Sometimes government gestures in this direction but simultaneously sends disaffected 14 year-olds out to work-based learning. That so many are disaffected by their schooling could be overcome not only by changing that education in the directions we have indicated above but by establishing the assumption of full citizenship rights and responsibilities for all from 18. This has never been clearly instituted in the UK, unlike other countries—the U.S.A, for example. It would help towards bringing all young people in from the margins of society, instead of relegating half of them to a secondary labour market in the regions and inner cities.

For those who have been alienated by their previous schooling in an academic and competitive system, the opportunities afforded by a further two years in sixth form or college may have to have as little resemblance as possible to that previous schooling—which in any case will have to change, doing away with what remains of the outdated and academic National Curriculum and its associated competitive tests and league tables. The curriculum police, OfSTED, can go with it, saving its £236 million 2007 budget. Nationalising the exam boards that profit from the system would also save another £610 million a year as gauged by Price Waterhouse Coopers in 2003-4 (www.qca.org.uk/2586_12129.html). Adequate financial support should then be available to students from the age of 16 onwards in order to raise participation rates and the rate of return post-18. Education Maintenance Allowances are a step forward but should be available to all.

As we have said, student fees must be abolished as this only deters many people who are unwilling to become indebted from entering higher education. Adequate maintenance is required so that students have time to pursue their studies and do not have to work their way through college or university unless they want to study part-time, for which option more allowances should also be made. Access courses should be extended and people's prior experiences recognised as entitling them to pursue their cultural and intellectual interests whether or not these are related to their employment. A learning entitlement on adequate grant maintenance will be expensive but it is a social priority required to raise the general level of learning amongst the population that is necessary for modernisation of the economy as well as to adapt to the accelerating pace of historical and climatic change.

This book has emphasised the interconnection not only between the various parts of what we argue is now an integrated compulsory and post-compulsory education and training system, but between that education system and other parts of society, particularly in relation to class and the economy. As a result, beginning to rethink education in the way that we have proposed will also invariably lead to discussions about other more substantial changes in society. For example, seeking to make education a form of liberation, rather than a means social control, will inevitably raise more general questions about the future of society and the need for alternatives to those offered by government, the CBI, the Bank of England, the European Union, the OECD, World Bank and World Trade Organisation. Likewise, democratising education in the way that we consider necessary is likely to lead to calls for the democratisation of other areas of society, while encouraging the development of an inquisitive and critical view of the workplace can only prompt changes in the way that work and economy are organised.

Simply, education can no longer be about selection for the employment hierarchy. We can learn from work but not necessarily just to work. The 'demands' of industry have to be set in a wider framework of human cultural and environmental need. If education is to build the skills and knowledge base of society to take fullest advantage of the latest developments in technology, it must begin by recognising how new technology has been applied during economic restructuring by the new market-state to deskill many of the tasks involved in production, distribution and services.

This book has described how old divisions have been supplanted by new. In particular, alongside a carnival of conspicuous consumption in an Americanised society where the rich disappear to second homes in the country and white flight takes to the suburbs or locks itself away in gated communities, an 'underclass' is stigmatized by a new poverty of low wages and casualised employment, disenfranchised from equal participation in society. We have emphasised that this development is linked to a real crisis for those now in 'the middle' of this newly redivided society. They are desperate for their children to avoid relegation to the new lumpen proletariat but prolonged participation in education does not guarantee secure employment in an economy where skill levels are rapidly subsumed as jobs can be outsourced to different continents and in a society where the traditional welfare safety net has been diminished and trade union power undermined. Constantly seeking to test, differentiate and marginalise students, schools, colleges and universities have played a large part in reinforcing this crisis, while the fifty per cent target for higher education—in so far as it is still adhered to—would, as we commented, still write off half the population.

The surrender of democratic control to the market has to be jettisoned in favour of an education which rejects the academic-vocational divisions with which we have been re-saddled since the 1988 Education Act.

To prevent the social isolation of an 'underclass', to preserve critical space at all levels of learning and counter 'dumbing down', to reverse privatisation of public service education and maintain free provision, so as to remain true to the Enlightenment ideal of understanding in order to control society and adapt it to its natural environment, a new direction at all levels of education and training is required.

References

References

Ainley, P. (1999) *Learning policy: Towards the certified society*, Basingstoke: Macmillan.

Ainley, P. (1994) *Degrees of difference: Higher education in the 1990s*, London: Lawrence and Wishart.

Ainley, P. and Bailey, B. (1997) *The business of learning: Staff and student experiences of further education in the 1990s*, London: Continuum.

Anderson, B. and Hatcher, R. (2005) Labour's transformation of the school system in England, in *Education's iron cage*, Canadian Centre for Policy Alternatives, Ottawa.

Aronowitz, S. and DiFazio, W. (1994) *The jobless future: Sci-tech and the dogma of work*, Minnesota: University of Minnesota Press

Ball, S. (forthcoming) *Education, Education, Education Policy*, Bristol: Policy Press.

Ball, S. (2003) *Class strategies and the education market: The middle classes and social advantage*, London: RoutledgeFalmer.

Barnett, R. (2003) *Beyond all reason: Living with ideology in the university*, Buckingham: The Society for Research into Higher Education and Open University Press.

Beckett, F. (2007) *The great city academy fraud*, London: Continuum.

Benn, C. and Chitty, C. (1996) *Thirty years on is comprehensive education alive and well or struggling to survive?* London: Fulton.

Benn, M. and Millar, F. (2006) *A comprehensive future*, London: Compass.

Brown, P., Hesketh, A. and Williams, S. (2004) *The mismanagement of talent, employability and jobs in the knowledge economy*, Oxford: Oxford University Press.

Bynner, J., Dolton, P., Feinstein, L., Makepiece, G., Malmberg, L. and Woods, L. (2003) *Revisiting the benefits of higher education*, London: HEFCE.

Canaan, J. and Ainley, P. (2005) Critical hope in English higher education today, constraints and possibilities in two new universities, *Teaching in Higher Education*, 10(4/October): 435-446.

Castells, M. (1996) *The rise of network society*, Oxford: Blackwell.

Chitty, C. (2004a) *Education policy in Britain*, Basingstoke: Palgrave Macmillan.

Chitty, C. (2004b) Eugenic theories and concepts of ability, in Benn, M. and Chitty, C. (eds) *A Tribute to Caroline Benn: Education and democracy*, London: Continuum.

Coard, B. (1971) *How the West Indian child is made educationally subnormal in the British school system*, London: New Beacon Press.

Cole, M. (1999) Globalisation, modernisation and New Labour, in Allen, M., Benn,C., Chitty,C., Cole, M., Hatcher, R., Hirtt, N. and Rikowski, G. (eds) *Business, business, business, New Labour's education policy*, London: the Tufnell Press.

Collins, R. (1979) *The credential society*, New York: Academic Press.

Confederation of British Industry, (CBI) (2006) *Working on the three Rs: Employers' priorities for functional skills in maths and English*, London: CBI

Cruddas, J. (2006) Neo-classical Labour, *Renewal*, 14(1 May) www.renewal.org.uk/issues/vol14no12006neoclassicallabour.asp

Dale, R. (1990) *The TVEI story*, Milton Keynes: Open University Press.

DES (1987) *The national curriculum 5-16*, London: DES.

DfEE (1992) *Choice and diversity*, London: DfEE.

DfEE (1997) *Excellence in schools*, London: HMSO.

DfES (2001) *Schools—Building on success*, London: HMSO

DfES (2002) *14-19: Extending opportunities, raising standards*, London: HMSO.

DfES (2002) *Schools—Achieving success*, London: HMSO.

DfES (2003) *Every child matters*, London: HMSO.

DfES (2005) *Higher standards—better schools for all*, London: HMSO.

Department of Health (2006) *Better doctors, safer patients*, London: DoH.

Dewey, J. (1966) *Democracy and Education*, Free Press: New York.

Ecclestone, K. (2002) *Learning autonomy in post-16 education: The politics and practice of formative assessment*, London: RoutledgeFalmer.

Ehrenreich, B. (2002) *Nickel and dimed: On not getting by in America*, New York: Henry Holt.

Evans, M. (2004) *Killing thinking, the death of the universities*, London: Continuum.

Evans, G. (2006) *Educational failure and working class white children in Britain*, Basingstoke: PalgraveMacmillan.

Felstead, A., Gallie, D. and Green, F. (2002) *Work skills in Britain 1986-2000*, Nottingham, DfES.

Finn, D. (1987) *Training without jobs, new deals and broken promises*, London: Macmillan.

Flett, K. (2007) *Chartism after 1848: The working class and the politics of radical education*, Monmouth: The Merlin Press.

Floud, J., Halsey, A. and Martin, F. (1956) *Social class and educational opportunity*, London: Heinemann.

Foster, A. (2005) *Realising the potential, A review of the future role of further education colleges*, Nottingham: DfES.

Furedi, F. (2004) *Where have all the intellectuals gone? Confronting 21st century philistinism*, London: Continuum.

Gamble, A. (1988) *The free economy and the strong state*, Basingstoke: Macmillan

Gillborn, D. and Mirza, H. (2000) *Educational inequality: Mapping race, class and gender: A synthesis of research evidence*, London: Office for Standards in Education.

Grant, N. (2005) *Hands off our schools! London:* Ealing Teachers Association.

Greenslade, R. (1976) *Goodbye to the working class*, London: Boyars.

HMSO (1967) *Children and their primary schools* (The Plowden Report), London: HMSO.

HMSO (1963) *Higher education* (The Robbins Report), London: HMSO.

HMSO (1963) *Half our future*, (The Newsom Report), London: HMSO.

The Hillcole Group (1997) *Rethinking education and democracy*, London: the Tufnell Press.

The Hillcole Group (1991) *Changing the future: Redprint for education*, London: the Tufnell Press.

Hills, J. and Stewart, K. (2005) *A more equal society? New Labour, poverty, inequality and exclusion*, Bristol: Policy Press.

Hirst, P. and Peters, R. (1966) *The logic of education*, London: Routledge.

Jackson, B. and Marsden, D. (1962) *Education and the working class: Some general themes raised by a study of 88 working-class children in a northern industrial city*, London: Routledge.

John, G. (2005) Parental and community involvement in education: time to get the balance right, in Richardson, B. (ed) *Tell it like it is: How our schools fail black children*, London: Bookmarks.

Jones, K. (2003) *Education in Britain 1944 to the present*, Cambridge: Polity.

Jones, K. (1989) *Right Turn, The Conservative revolution in education*, London: Hutchinson.

Jones, K. (1983) *Beyond progressive education*, London: Macmillan.

Learning and Skills Council (2003) *Further education and work-based learning for young people—Learner numbers in England: 2002/2003*, Coventry: LSC.

Leys, C. (2001) *Market-driven politics, neoliberal democracy and the public interest*, London: Verso.

Mizen, P. (2004) *The changing state of youth*, Basingstoke: PalgraveMacmillan.

Mortimore, P. (2006) *Which way forward?* London: NUT .

NUT (1990) *A strategy for the curriculum*, London: NUT.

NUT (2005) *Breaking down the barriers*, London: NUT.

Nolan, K. and Anyon, J. (2004) Learning to do time: Willis's model of cultural reproduction in an era of postindustrialism, globalisation, and mass incarceration, in Dolby, N. and Dimitriadis G. (eds) *Learning to labor in new times*, New York: RoutledgeFalmer.

The Nuffield Foundation (2006) *Third annual report*, London: The Nuffield Foundation.

Organisation for Economic Cooperation and Development (1988) *The future of social protection*, Paris: OECD.

Organisation for Economic Cooperation and Development (2006) *Education at a glance 2006*, Paris: OECD.

Pollock, A. (2004) *NHS plc, The privatisation of our health care*, London: Verso.

Postman, N. and Weingartner, C. (1969) *Teaching as a subversive activity*, New York: Dell.

Pugsley, L. (2004) *The university challenge: Higher education markets and social stratification*, Aldershot: Ashgate.

Reay, D. and Wiliam, D (1999) "I'll be a nothing": Structure, agency and the construction of identity through assessment, *British Educational Research Journal*, 25(3): 343-354.

Rikowski, G. (2006) The long moan of history: Employers on school leavers, *The Volumizer*, journals.aol.co.uk/rikowskigr/Volumizer

Roberts,K. (2000) *Class in modern Britain*, Basingstoke: Macmillan.

Robbins, D. (1988) *The rise of independent study, the politics and philosophy of an educational innovation 1970-87*, Milton Keynes: Open University Press and the Society for Research into Higher Education.

Robinson, E. (1968) *The new polytechnics: The people's universities*, Harmondsworth: Penguin.

Roy, W. (1968) *The Teachers' Union*, London: Schoolmaster Publishing Company.

Ryan, A. (2006) New Labour and higher education, in Walford, G. (ed) *Education and the Labour Government, An evaluation of two terms*, Abingdon: Routledge.

Shayer, M. forthcoming, *British Journal of Educational Psychology*.

Shumar, W. (1997) *College for sale, a critique of the commodification of higher education*, London: Falmer.

s.i. Marcos (2000) *Our word is our weapon, selected writings subcomandante Marcos* edited and translated by Juana Ponce de Leon, New York: Seven Stories Press.

Socialist Movement Education Group (1990) *Education, towards a socialist perspective*, London: SMEG.

Stern, N. (2007) *Review on the economics of climate change*, Cambridge: Cambridge University Press and also www.hm-treasury.gov.uk/independent_reviews/stern_review_economics_climate_change/stern_review_report.cfm

Sutton Trust (2005) *Intergenerational mobility in Europe and North America*, London: The Sutton Trust.

Tomlinson, S. (2005) *Education in a post-welfare society*, Buckingham: Open University Press.

Toynbee, P. (2003) *Hard work: Life in low-pay Britain*, London: Bloomsbury.

Warnock, M. (2005) *Special educational needs: A new look*, London: Philosophy of Education Society Impact Booklet 11.

Whitfield, D. (2006) *New Labour's attack on public services*, Nottingham: Spokesman.

Whitfield, D. (2001) *Public services or corporate welfare: Rethinking the nation state in the global economy*, London: Pluto.

Willis, P. (1977) *Learning to Labour: How working class kids get working class jobs*, Aldershot: Saxon House.

Wilmott, P. and Young, M. (1957) *Family and kinship in east London*, London: Routledge.

Wolf, A. (2003) *Does education matter?* Harmondsworth: Penguin.

Wrigley,T. (2006) *Another school is possible*, London: Bookmarks.

Young, M.D. (ed) (1971) *Knowledge and control: New directions for the sociology of education*, London: Macmillan.

Socialist Education Journal, www.socialist-teacher.org, and

Post-16 Educator, post16educator.googlepages.com, provide consistent sources of reference with relevant articles by the authors and others.

Index

Employers, labour markets, FE, HE, schools (primary and secondary), teachers and lecturers, pupils and students throughout. For New and Old Labour/ Conservative governments and Parties see Thatcher, Blair, Wilson etc..

Printed in the United Kingdom
by Lightning Source UK Ltd.
122967UK00001B/263/A